Recreation and Fitness Facilities

Planning, Design, and Construction

By: Betty Montgomery

Sagamore Publishing

a division of
Management Learning Laboratories

Published by:	Sagamore Publishing a division of Management Learning Laboratories 302 W. Hill Champaign, IL 61820
Design by:	Susan M. Williams
Artwork:	Kelly Day
Printed by:	Braun-Brumfield, Ann Arbor, MI
Copyright:	© Sagamore Publishing, 1988

Library of Congress Card No.: 88-61738
ISBN: 0-915611-18-X

The information contained herein provides general principles and guidelines for the construction and/or renovation of a recreation and sports complex. Since the actual construction and/or renovation of individual projects will vary, it is recommended that users of this information consult further with architects, engineers, and other appropriate resources before beginning projects.

To

My Father

Acknowledgements

I would like to express my appreciation to the many generous people who shared their knowledge and expertise with me in the preparation of this book. Howard Kessler and Bill Merci (Kessler, Merci and Associates) and Jim Flynn (Hastings and Chivetta) three architects who have dedicated their time and talent to the construction and renovation of recreation and fitness/wellness facilities have shared materials and ideas with me.

I could never have completed this project without the support and contributions of my friends and colleagues in the Office of Campus Recreation at Northern Illinois University. Their patience and encouragement is greatly appreciated.

I particularly want to thank David Miller (Hastings and Chivetta) who has shared in the excitement and frustration of each chapter over the last two years. Not only has he been an endless well of information, but also a friend. Along with David, Kurt Carmen (Southern Illinois University) encouraged me and also contributed to the success of this endeavor.

The contributions of manufacturers and distributors of various materials and products provided much of the current information in this book. I wish to thank all of them, for without their generosity this book could not have been written. Likewise a special thanks is extended to the many professionals who spent time showing me around their facilities.

And finally to Joe Bannon, (Sagamore Publishing) and Kelly Day, illustrator for this book, I owe sincere thanks for their encouragement and support.

Foreword

The information found in this book will serve as a practical guide for the construction, renovation and operation of recreation and fitness/wellness facilities. In addition to being used by professional planners and practitioners it may also function as a textbook for college and university courses which are designed to prepare students in recreation, physical education and fitness/wellness related fields.

The text is divided into three sections: Planning and the Wellness Concept, Construction, and Operation.

Section I addresses the wellness movement and the planning process involved in constructing a facility which will house a recreation or fitness/wellness program. Chapter 2 specifically focuses on utilization of strategic planning, beginning with "establishing a mission" and carrying through the process to "ensuring implementability" of the project.

Section II includes chapters which address types of surfaces used in construction, a comparison of these surfaces and also descriptions and comparisons of various types of lighting. Chapters are also included which offer an overview of individual areas, i.e. gymnasiums, racquetball/handball courts, weight/exercise rooms, areas for creative expression, swimming pools, outdoor equipment and resource centres, locker rooms and public rest rooms, service areas, and various miscellaneous areas.

Section III focuses on the operation of the facility. Chapter 14 deals with maintenance issues, e.g. design of service areas, staffing, equipment and supplies and methods for cleaning special surfaces.

This book is by no means the last word in construction and operation of facilities, but if I have accomplished what I intended to, it will serve as a good source of basic information for the practitioner and the student as well as a guide for the professional planner.

Table of Contents

Section I: Planning and the Wellness Concept

Section II: Construction

Section III: Operations

WELLNESS AND

THE PLANNING PROCESS

Section I

The first section of this book introduces the reader to the wellness concept and its growing popularity over the past few years. With this concept in mind, the strategic planning of construction or renovation of recreation and fitness/wellness facilities is explored.

1 Recreation and the Wellness Concept

It is clear that recreation has become a major focus of life in our society. It is "in" to play. The positive attitude toward recreation has been heightened by the public's growing awareness of the importance of a healthy body. This awareness became apparent to the American society in the late 1950s after President Eisenhower suffered a heart attack. His physician, Dr. Paul Dudley White, prescribed mild exercise through a recreational activity, golf, to aid in his recuperation. White turned attention to the fact that exercise is needed in all phases of life. "Physical fitness" became a popular concept to millions of Americans. Today we continue to seek high levels of physical fitness through leisure time activities, but we have come to realize that it is equally important to seek high levels of psychological and emotional well-being.

In the 1950s, while attention was being called to President Eisenhower's rehabilitation, Dr. Halbert L. Dunn, a retired public health physician was introducing the concept of "high level wellness." He defined wellness as "an integrated method of functioning that is oriented toward maximizing the potential of the individual within his or her particular environment." He stressed the holistic nature of wellness and set the stage for those to follow who would offer other definitions. Their common belief was that good health meant not only physical well being but also other dimensions of well-being, eg. psychological, sociological, emotional, and spiritual.

It is apparent that the American lifestyle is generally not a healthy one. We eat too much,

The desire to stay healthy has become a key focal point for Americans over the last two decades. (photo: Gustavus Adolphus College, courtesy of Hastings & Chivetta Architects)

drink too much, smoke, manage stress poorly and probably do not exercise nearly enough. However, the ongoing need to become healthy and stay healthy has emerged as a key focal point for millions of Americans over the last two decades. In this country over 30 million people engage in regular, active walking for exercise. An additional seventeen million run. Membership in the YMCA has increased nearly 20 percent over the last decade, while attendance in exercise classes conducted at "Ys" jumped nearly 30 percent in five years. While YMCAs are increasing their membership, fitness and racquet clubs are also vying for their business. Hotels and multi-unit housing developments now offer full service recreation facilities for their occupants. New residential developments are likewise offering potential buyers on-site clubs and facilities as part of their total package.

The rising costs in health care have stimulated the interest in improving health through changing lifestyle. Americans spend billions of dollars each year on illnesses that might have been prevented. Today more and more doctors are prescribing exercise as a way to increase overall health and reduce the risk of developing serious illnesses, especially heart disease. Thousands of hospitals are promoting good health practices through programming and through construction of fitness facilities within the hospital grounds.

The interest in staying healthy is further encouraged by the employer who is discovering that it is more economical to keep the employee healthy than it is to pay for illnesses.

Companies are demonstrating their concern through provision of programs on nutrition, smoking, alcohol and drug abuse and providing exercise facilities for the employee.

Americans spend $255 billion yearly on recreation and recreational products. This amounts to $1 out of every $9 spent by the typical American household. In the past ten years bookstores have doubled their inventory of literature dealing with fitness, wellness, good health practices and specific sports activities. The National Sporting Goods Association reported that annual sales of athletic equipment increased from $3.6 billion to more than $5 billion in two years.

The increased interest in personal fitness has created a need for additional facilities. Existing facilities are becoming more crowded and demands are being placed on municipal recreation concerns, colleges and universities, public and private schools, private clubs, business and industry, hospitals, and senior citizens facilities to create space for engaging in wellness related programs. In response to these demands, the 1980s have become the decade for construction of these facilities.

The primary thrust of the wellness movement has largely been in terms of lifestyle issues such as fitness, diet, and stress management. Most of the attention in the literature of the wellness movement has focused on motivating individuals to take responsibility for personal behaviors and attitudes in order to promote healthier, more fulfilling lives. Less attention has been given to the ways in which the environment, (particularly the physical environment) influences human behaviors and attitudes, and consequently, wellness outcomes. The physical environment created for recreation and fitness/wellness facilities is especially important, therefore the development of these facilities provides a rare

Libraries, for example, are typically designed to promote a quiet, well-lit, comfortable environment which is conducive to cerebral activities. In much the same way, it is important to have facilities which provide the optimum conditions for promoting wellness behaviors and

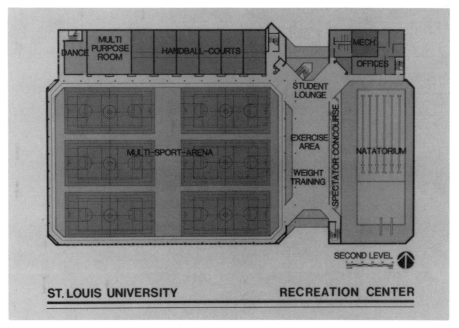

The increased interest in fitness has led to a need for new recreation/fitness facilities.
(photo: St. Louis Recreation Center, courtesy Hastings & Chivetta Architects, Inc.)

opportunity to create the kind of physical environment and supporting programs which will encourage the development of wellness behavior and values.

Extensive research has been conducted on the impact of various features of the environment upon attitudes and behaviors. Factors such as color, use of space, lighting, type of furniture, and background noise, all have subtle and sometimes even profound impacts on behavior and feelings. Ideally, physical facilities are specifically designed to promote the human behaviors and values which are the objectives of the activities housed therein.

values. These facilities can be a focal point, a visible symbol, of the institution's or agency's concern for, and commitment to wellness.

Recreation and fitness/wellness facilities should be designed to accommodate programs which reflect a philosophy of total well-being. Such facilities must provide opportunities for creative expression, social interaction, mental stimulation, rest and relaxation, as well as a variety of opportunities for physical fitness. A wellness-oriented facility must be functionally designed to provide a safe, healthful, and attractive environment in which individuals have an opportunity to enjoy a wide range of leisure interests and needs.

An attractive and functional recreation or fitness/wellness facility can provide space in the community where families can engage in healthy activities together. It can serve as a recruitment tool for business and industry as well as for educational institutions. Statistics indicate that a well planned facility will contribute to productivity, morale, and employee longevity. In conclusion, an attractive environment conducive to wellness activity can open a whole new world to the potential user. Imagination and initiative followed by careful planning can eventually transform a vision into reality.

Selected Bibliography

Ardell, D. (1982). *Planning for wellness.* Dubuque: Kendall/Hunt.

Crawford, A. (1987, November) Recreation facility design: planning from paper to plaster. *Journal of Employee Recreation, Health and Education*, p.9

Flynn, R. (1987, March). Tracking trends in facility design. *Athletic Business*, pp. 32-35

Gregory, R. (1987, February) Recreation facility construction. *Journal of Employee Recreation, Health and Education, p.26.*

Is America an island of facility design? (1986, December). *Athletic Business*, pp.18-25.

Montgomery, B., and Dalton, J. (1986). Promoting wellness through recreation facility development and programming. In F. Leafgren (Ed.), *Developing campus recreation and wellness programs.* (pp. 43-52). San Francisco: Jossey-Bass.

Total wellness: the new market in club services. (1985, April). *Athletic Business*, pp.42-44.

2

Planning the Project

Planning is an intellectually demanding process that gets us from where we are to where we want to be.

• A director of a campus recreation program is asked by the vice president to participate in the development of a plan to design a new recreation facility.

• A manager of a unit within a large corporation is assigned the task of investigating the possibility of converting a area of an existing facility into a health club for employees.

• An area coordinator for a local park district is assigned the task of assessing the needs of the community regarding a new building that will house racquetball courts.

• A member of a hospital staff is called upon to work with a committee whose task is to design a new cardiac rehabilitation center.

All these situations occur in a different setting, however, they have one common characteristic. All involve some level of planning for the renovation or construction of recreation or fitness/wellness facilities.

The planning process, the most basic of all administrative functions, helps us decide *what* is to be done; *when* it is to be done; *how* it should be done; and *who* is to perform the task. Long-range planning provides an opportunity to simulate the future. The construction or renovation of recreation or fitness/wellness facilities begins with this process. However, long-range plans often become a wish list of things to be accomplished if certain circumstances exist, such as available funding. Unfortunately these plans are often taken from the shelf periodically, dusted off and carefully returned until another time. Strategic planning, on the other hand, denotes a process whereby commitment is given to resources to gain an objective. Strategic planning denotes action and must be employed before the project is undertaken. It includes establishing a mission, selecting objectives, setting goals, analyzing strengths and weaknesses, studying threats to the plan, preparing the planning document, and ensuring implementability.

Establishing a mission

In the case of building a new, or renovating an existing facility, assessing the need of the participants will help determine what is needed and thus help in establishing the mission. A survey of leisure behavior and attitudes developed by the sponsoring agency, can be used to determine the needs and desires of the potential users and can later be used to assist in developing an effective marketing strategy. To survey the potential users an instrument which asks for simple responses should be developed. Information gathered from this survey should help in developing a mission statement.

> **Mission Statement**
> The (name of agency) provides a comprehensive wellness program which incorporates fitness, diet, and stress management. (name of agency)'s purpose is to construct a wellness facility that will accommodate these programs and reflect a philosophy of total well-being.

Selecting objectives

A survey will allow for analysis of demographic characteristics, availability of existing activities, behavior patterns and opinions regarding the provisions of programs and facilities. Survey results provide data for a comprehensive facility and program plan and help determine specific objectives.

Setting goals

Ideally, a facility should be dedicated to serving all members of the agency or institution. Therefore, it must provide for multiple use at reasonable cost to the participant, and it must be easily supervised, maintained and well-

located. The goal then is to provide such a facility.

Analyzing strengths and weaknesses

The planning process requires capitalizing on strengths and eliminating weaknesses. If strengths lie in the availability of experts, these individuals should be involved in the planning process. Likewise including influential persons may be a significant strength in reaching the final goal, especially if these individuals have a vested interest in the project.

On the other hand, an overabundance of self-proclaimed experts may surface as a profound weakness. An effort should be made to avoid, whenever possible, including these individuals in the planning process. Their "expertise" will undoubtedly surface as a weakness and the effects of their lack of knowledge will eventually add additional cost to the project.

Threats to the plan

Funding often becomes a major issue and a threat to the plan. In considering funding of a new facility, a financial profile of projected income and expenditures must be developed. This financial profile or plan must be developed in cooperation with the institution's or agency's fiscal officers, a selected architectural firm and a banking agency. It should include annual financial requirements, projected operating revenue, sources of operating revenue, and if applicable, projected enrollment of the institution and proposed user fees which could provide the basic financial support.

Prepare the planning document

The need for sound planning and justification of a new facility are obviously imperative. Participation is strategic and essential in generating wide-spread support. Potential users, recreation and fitness/wellness personnel, administrators, consultants, maintenance staff and representatives from other pertinent groups should contribute ideas. The major task of a planning committee is to generate and refine ideas and to advise individuals responsible for developing a program statement. It is important for a facility planning group to visit other benchmark facilities and confer with other professionals and users. These visits will assist the committee with planning and help them avoid making costly budgeting mistakes.

The program statement is the document that is used to communicate the needs of the institution or agency to the architect. It should include a description of current and anticipated programs and a detailed account of existing facilities used in the recreation or fitness program, the range of users, scheduling of the facility, features noted at other facilities, and any other activities the building might be used for. In addition to these considerations, key factors that will ensure more efficient operation of the facility include the following:

1.   **Maximum utilization of space.** Whenever practical, plan the facilities so they have multiple use. Multi-purpose gymnasiums can accommodate a number of activities such as basketball, volleyball, badminton, tennis and jogging. A suitable multi-purpose surface will allow other activities as well. Floor hockey, indoor soccer and other field games can be accommodated. Activity rooms with hardwood floors may be used for aerobic dance and other dance forms, meetings, an audio-visual projection area, and martial arts.

2.   **Traffic flow and circulation.** The facility should be designed so that major activity areas are independent and self-contained. Participants engaging in one activity should not be disturbed by activities or traffic in adjacent areas. For instance if perimeters of gymnasiums are used for housing weight machines and exercise equipment, a problem may result when traffic passes through one area to get to the other. Likewise noise from either area may disturb activities in the other. Many new designs include such utilization of space. Whereas it may address some concerns it will create the problem of difficult circulation and intense traffic flow.

3.   **Supervisory needs.** Designing a building that is easily supervised will facilitate management and will be appreciated by the participant. The administrative office and the service desk should be located near the main entrance of the building where flow of traffic entering and exiting the building may be viewed. Depending on the size of the building, additional supervisory stations may be included. A glass enclosed area adjacent to a large gymnasium can serve several purposes. Supervisor's stations are covered in greater detail in Chapter 5.

4.   **Management costs.** Choose materials and equipment that are easily maintained. In the long run, this is a major cost-saving consideration. Clean, attractive facilities

are more conducive to participation and promote a more positive experience.

Ensure implementability

The first step toward ensuring implementability is to select and hire the architect. The names of prominent firms will surface during visits to other facilities. Other names for consideration can be obtained from professional journals, trade magazines and conferences where firms display exhibits. After a list has been compiled the committee should select a few firms that will be asked to submit a Statement of Interest and Qualifications (SIQ) (Appendix A). From these responses a short list is developed, and a Request for Proposal (RFP) (see Appendix B) is sought from firms on the short list. The RFP is much more detailed than the SIQ, therefore the architect and the interviewing agency often prefer to spend time preparing and reviewing this document with a few potential firms. After RFPs have been submitted, the firms are invited for interviews. Sample questions and evaluation criteria are found in Appendix C & D.

Choosing the right architect is one of the most crucial decisions made in a project. In addition to possessing technical skills and design ideas which are compatible with those technical skills and design ideas which are compatible with those of the institutions or agency, the architects should be able to works effectively with the planning committee. The relationships that develop between the architectural representatives and the client are very important because of frequent contact and communication.

The architect's responsibilities include pre-design planning, developing a schematic design, converting the program statement into graphic representation of the building plan, developing the design, preparing construction documents, orchestrating the bidding process, and supervising the construction through completion.

The final step in ensuring implementability is the construction or renovation of the facility. This is by far the most exciting phase of the planning process. Witnessing the culmination of a well-designed plan which will accommodate programs that reflect the philosophy of the institution or agency is a very rewarding experience. In fact, the construction process should be enjoyable. The final success of the project depends greatly on the interaction and communication between the architect, contractor and user. It is imperative, therefore, that representatives from these groups meet on a regular basis throughout the construction phase.

Without proper facilities it is difficult if not impossible to promote wellness behavior or the wise use of leisure time. Consequently, it is essential that recreation and fitness/wellness facilities become a strategic means for encouraging participants to become involved in activities that will enhance their lives. These facilities must be aesthetically pleasing, well maintained and also functional.

Because of the emphasis on visual aspects of the facility, a tremendous number of new products have become available in recent years. The manufacturers of these products concentrate on beautification and function. In the following chapters, these products will be examined.

Selected Bibliography

Bannon, J. (1985) *Leisure resources: its comprehensive planning* . Champaign, IL.: Management Learning Laboratories.

Council of Educational Facility Planners,International. (1985). *Guide for planning educational facilities.* Columbus, OH.: Author.

Flynn, R., (ed.) (1985) *Planning facilities for athletics and physical education and recreation.* Athletic Institute and AAHPERD.

Hammitt, S. & Hammitt, W. (1985, January) Campus Recreation Facilities: Planning for Better use. *JOHPERD*, p.23.

Kendall, K., McGregor, I., & Gamble, B. (1982) Strategic Planning: an Essential tool for surviving in the eighties. *Process and concepts in recreation sports.* pp.60-85.

Lewis, M. & Nelson, M. (1982). How to work with an architect. *Wilson Library Bulletin,* 57 (1), pp. 444-46

Norris, D. & Poulton, N. (1987). *A guide for new planners.* Ann Arbor: The Society for College and University Planning.

Penman, K. (1977). *Planning physical education and athletic facilities in schools.* New York: John Wiley and Sons.

Planning facilities for athletics, physical education, and recreation. (1977). Washington,D.C. : The Athletic Institute and The America Alliance for Health, Physical Education, Recreation and Dance.

Ribaric, R. (1987, March). Don't get ambushed by costly surprises. *Athletic Business,* pp.46-47.

Secor, M. (1983). Where do we want the outlets? In B. Vendl, L. Hisaka, W. Holsberry, G. Maas, M. Stevenson (Eds.), *Toward an understanding of intramural-recreational sports,* pp.342-350.

Tully D. (1980, November). Decision making in the planning process. *Athletic Business 10,* pp.16-19.

CONSTRUCTION

Section II

This section is concerned with the construction of recreation and fitness/wellness facilities. Suggestions will be made which pertain to design, choice of materials, product types, etc. These suggestions are merely that, and are based on the author's experience, review of current literature and observation of renovated and newly constructed facilities. The reader must keep in mind that the situation often dictates the choice and there is no single perfect way.

3

Surfaces

FLOORING

It has been said many times and it is worth repeating, that no single floor surface is ideal for all the activities it must accommodate. Therefore, in choosing a multi-use surface, careful consideration should be given to factors which affect all programs, (e.g. performance, cost, maintenance, durability.) Choice can become confusing when manufacturers claim their product costs less, is easier to maintain, is more durable and ensures top quality performance. To complicate matters even more, the market is flooded with many innovative floor surfaces. All claim to be different, but in fact many are similar in performance, cost, maintenance requirements and durability. The differences are in the composition of the material and the manner in which they are installed.

In choosing floor surfaces for both playing areas and other areas of a facility it is important to choose the type of material that best suits the individual situation. This chapter includes descriptions of materials that will help in the selection of appropriate floor surfaces. They include wood, synthetic materials, carpeting, and various types of tile.

Playing Surfaces

Wood

The maple floor has been the most popular and preferred playing surface for many years. Athletes and coaches "swear" by it and recreation professionals prefer it for many activities. It is the single most popular floor for basketball, volleyball, racquetball/handball, and dance activities.

Several different floor anchoring systems allow for versatility. The *mastic set floor* (figure 3-1) provides a low profile surface and can be installed directly onto existing floor surfaces or onto concrete in a new facility. This surface is suitable for bearing heavy loads. Although it is inexpensive, it is a poor installation for resiliency.

The *anchored channel system* (figure 3-2) provides a fast playing surface. In this system the hardwood floor surface is held together by steel clips and is channel mounted. It is more resistant to high humidity than a mastic set floor. It is also suitable for bearing heavy loads.

Still another system, the *anchored sleeper*, (figure 3-3) is a high profile system with excellent shock absorbing characteristics. In this system the "sleeper" is placed over a concrete base. The hardwood surface is then nailed to a cushiony material, the sleeper. This system creates a slower playing surface than the previously mentioned systems.

The *floating sleeper*, (figure 3-4) also a high profile system, differs from the anchored sleeper in that a softwood subfloor is placed between the cushiony material and hardwood surface. This feature adds strength and rigidity to the surface.

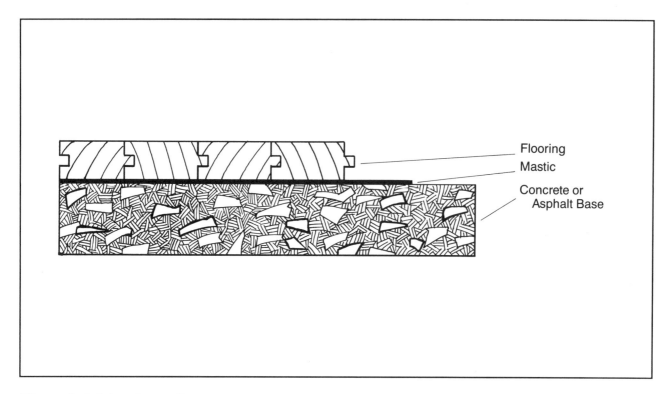

Figure 3-1: Mastic set floor

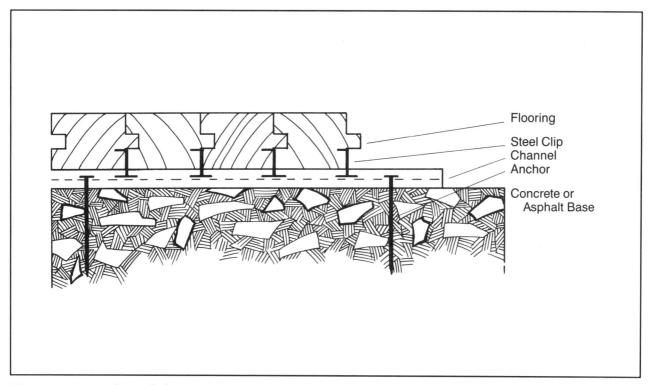

Figure 3-2: Anchored channel system

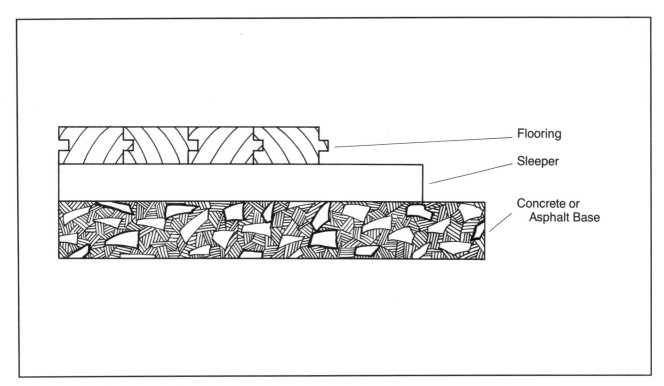

Figure 3-3: Anchored sleeper

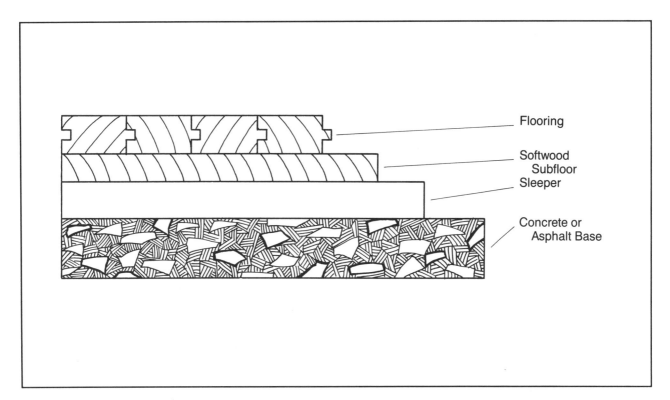

Figure 3-4: Floating sleeper

The hardwood surface is a high performance surface. It provides true ball response, good rebound and no bite or spin, an action which occurs on many synthetic surfaces. It is shock absorbent and minimizes leg fatigue. Its durability is proven by the existence of many floors which are thirty, forty or fifty years old.

Whereas hardwood floors are easier to maintain today than they were several years ago, they must be refinished periodically and lines must also be repainted from time to time, depending on usage. Wood floors are probably not the best surface for large, heavy use areas where participants wear shoes that are also worn outside the facility.

Wood floors are not as versatile as many of the synthetic surfaces. They are poor surfaces for tennis courts and also do not provide a good surface for running tracks.

Poured in place

The liquid urethane surface is poured in place over concrete or asphalt and is allowed to cure (figure 3-5). It is a tough surface which withstands high humidity and will support heavy loads. Different textures may be obtained by adding a final coating to the surface. The poured in place, seam-free (monolithic) surface also allows for color choice and differentiation. Its smoothness and resiliency make it suitable

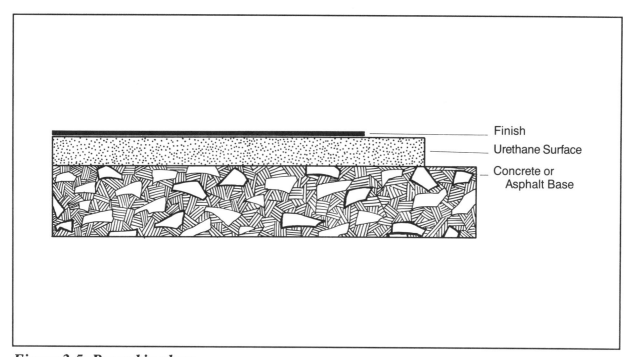

Finish

Urethane Surface

Concrete or
Asphalt Base

Figure 3-5: Poured in place

Hardwood floors resist normal humidity quite well, but will warp and buckle in instances where heavy humidity is a factor. Replacing flooring damaged by water or humidity can be a costly and time consuming task.

for basketball, volleyball, tennis and track.

Although the urethane surface is the choice of many recreation professionals, there are some disadvantages. If not installed properly the poured in place surface can show signs of cracking soon after installation. Because it is a liquid it conforms to the subsurface. If the concrete or asphalt base is not level, varying thicknesses will occur causing varying degrees of resiliency. Likewise any cracks or seams in the subsurface will eventually become cracks or seams in the surface.

The smoother finishes provide poor traction and are slippery when wet. They are also easily defaced. These facts may be of concern to the user if the surface is to be utilized as a multi-purpose area.

Whereas the urethane surface may be somewhat less expensive than other surfaces, the frequent replacing of top coating and repainting of lines may be expensive. In heavy use areas top coating and lines will need to be replaced often.

Similar to the poured in place surface, the *trowel applied* chemical composition floor provides a seamless surface with many of the same characteristics as the poured in place. The major difference is in the method of installation.

Pre-fab or Rolled

Pre-fabricated rubber flooring (figure 3-6) provides a tough, resilient surface. Finishes can range from smooth to varying degrees of texture. Rubber surfaces ensure true ball bounce and reduce leg fatigue. They are not slippery when wet. Rolled products have the advantage of uniformity in thickness and density, whereas poured products will vary.

The rolled surface may be less advantageous than the monolithic because of the seams between each installed piece. These seams have a tendency to separate over time and will also collect dirt. Some rubber products are very difficult to clean. Stains are hard to remove especially from lighter colored surfaces. Lines must also be repainted often.

Polyvinylchloride (PVC) is a prefabricated solid cast vinyl flooring. Like rubber sheet goods, it comes in rolls and is applied over concrete or asphalt with an adhesive. It is available in a variety of textures and colors. The participant will probably notice very little

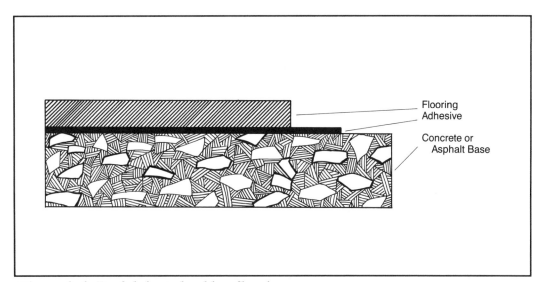

Figure 3-6: Prefabricated rubber flooring

difference in the performance between rubber and PVC flooring. The major difference lies in the composition of the material.

The chemicals in plastic materials often cause a displeasing odor. Plastics also have a tendency to harden and shrink. Shrinking will definitely open seams creating crevices that are aesthetically displeasing and difficult to clean. PVC flooring may require special products for removal of stains or heavy soil.

Carpet

Carpeting or soft surface is one of the newest and most innovative playing surfaces. Nylon pile fused to a vinyl backing provides a durable, low maintenance, versatile surface which is designed to give the same ball bounce

Carpeting is much easier to maintain than hard surfaces. Regular vacuuming and occasional shampooing are all that is required. Refinishing, resurfacing and relining are not necessary. Soft surfaces are acoustically far superior to hard surfaces.

As with all playing surfaces there are also disadvantages to carpeting. Some participants find the superior traction undesirable. Carpet burns often result from falls, however, floor burns can be sustained on wood, rubber or vinyl surfaces as well.

The *interlocking rubber tile system* (figure 3-7) allows installation without adhesive. It is primarily designed to absorb the shock and noise of heavy free weight equipment. In

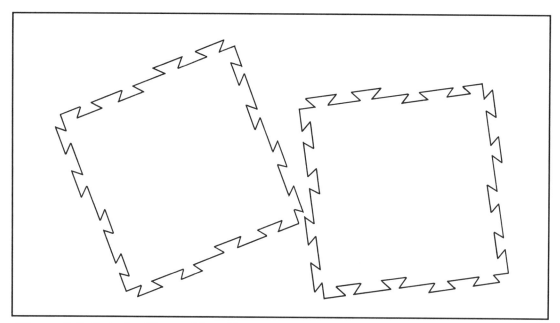

Figure 3-7: Interlocking rubber tile

response as the hard surfaces. Carpeting can be installed with a strong adhesive over any existing concrete, wood or vinyl floor. Lines are cut separately and are installed permanently. Proper installation will eliminate any seam lines.

addition to having all the characteristics of rolled rubber goods, individual tiles may be interchanged or even reversed.

Interlocking PVC tiles are used primarily in areas where floors get wet, e.g. pool decks, showers, locker rooms. However, manufacturers also recommend them for tennis courts, entry ways and weight-exercise rooms. They are easily installed and may be interchanged or replaced readily.

A disadvantage of interlocking tiles may be that they are easily removed and attractive to vandals and thieves. Constant replacement of tiles can be expensive and inconvenient. Additional seams also increase the crevices where dirt can accumulate.

A comparison of playing surfaces is shown in figure 3-8.

Other Surfaces

Hard Surfaces

Hard surface tile is easy to maintain but very difficult to install. It is brittle and inflexible and must be laid over a surface that is completely smooth and rigid. It may be laid over a wood floor but a good underlayment must be installed first. The best base for this is concrete.

Quarry tile is made from natural clay and makes an excellent surface for entry ways and hallways. It requires no special care other than daily maintenance. It is not slippery when wet.

Ceramic tile is an attractive surface for locker rooms and public toilets. It is also easy to maintain and requires no special care. Floor tiles with glazed finishes may be slippery when wet.

Terrazzo tile provides a long-wearing, attractive, low maintenance seamless floor. It never wears out and is therefore suitable for high traffic areas. Terrazzo is only as good as its substrate, therefore proper installation is essential to prevent cracking. It will degenerate under acid and consequently is not a good surface for toilet areas.

Resilient flooring

Resilient flooring includes both tiles and sheet goods. Tiles are less expensive, easier to install and are more resistant to dents from items such as desk and chair legs. Scuffs and scars will show and are sometimes difficult to remove.

Vinyl tiles provide a good surface for janitor closets, vending rooms, laundry rooms, leisure crafts labs or other areas where spills may occur. They are not the best surface for heavy traffic areas.

Carpeting

A tufted weave nylon carpet is a good choice for office floors. It is very durable and resistant to abrasion and mildew. Unibond carpeting has the backing material bonded to the surface and may be installed directly over a concrete base floor. Nylon carpeting should be treated for static electricity.

Other types of carpeting are often used in hallways. These pile-form or loop-form carpetlike materials are not woven as is nylon carpeting. Instead, they are embedded in a flexible, tough backing material. They are installed with an adhesive over a concrete base.

The best floor is the one that fits the situation best. No surface is perfect. All types have definite advantages and disadvantages. Regardless of choice, factors that should be

Figure 3-8

COMPARISON OF PLAYING SURFACES

Surface			Cost Comparison	Playability	Short Term Maintenance	Long Term Maintenance	Durability
Wood			Most Expensive	Good rebound characteristics. Excellent surface for basketball, volleyball/racquetball. Good traction.	Mop daily with dust mop.	Annual recoating. Frequent replacement of lines.	Proven record of longevity if properly maintained. Affected by humidity.
Poured in Place			Less expensive than rolled	Good rebound characteristics. Smooth surfaces are slippery when wet. Good surface for basketball, track, volleyball and tennis. Average traction.	Sweep daily. Considerable ongoing maintenance. Monolithic surface facilitates maintenance.	Requires expensive coating. Frequent replacement of lines. Easily defaced.	Cracks if not installed properly. Not affected by humidity.
Rolled	Rubber		More expensive than Poured in place	Good rebound characteristics. Good surface for basketball, track, Not as good for volleyball, tennis. Good traction.	Very difficult to clean. Stains easily. Vacuum daily.	Seams may separate. Frequent replacement of lines.	Very durable.
		PVC		Smooth surfaces are slippery when wet. Poor rebound characteristics. Adequate surface for tennis, track, volleyball, basketball.	Difficult to clean. Vulnerable to common cleaning agents. Sweep daily.	Becomes hard and brittle over time. Frequent replacement of lines.	Tough, wears well. May shrink, causing seams to separate.
Interlocking Tile	Rubber		Less expensive than Poured in place	Often used in weight rooms. Absorbs shock well.	Very difficult to clean. Dirt accumulates in seams. Vacuum daily.	Tiles may be preserved by interchanging. Easily replaced.	Corners and edges turn up. Easily removed-may be attractive to vandals.
		PVC		Used primarily in locker rooms, showers and pool decks.	Difficult to clean. Vulnerable to common cleaning agents.	Tiles may be preserved by interchanging. Easily replaced.	Corners and edges turn up. Easily removed-may be attractive to vandals.
Carpet			Least expensive of all	Good rebound characteristics. Good surface for basketball, track, tennis. Not good for volleyball. Positive traction.	Vacuum daily. Spot clean as needed.	Steam clean annually. No replacement of lines.	Durable, long lasting.

considered include: durability, playability, and maintenance.

Choices should not be made from catalogues and literature alone, but rather from visitations to other institutions and agencies. Testimonials from colleagues is the best source of information available.

Walls

With such a wide variety of materials available, the task of selecting wall surfaces may be as difficult as that of choosing floor surfaces. The same criteria should be considered, e.g. playability, durability, maintenance and cost.

The following types of wall surfaces will be discussed in this chapter: drywall, plaster, concrete, brick, foam core galvanized steel panels, melamine laminated panels, tile and wallcovering.

Drywall

The most popular of all interior wall surfaces is gypsum board or drywall, a sheet of plaster faced on both sides with paper. Drywall is often **the** wall used in the construction of aerobic/dance areas, offices, and hallways. Although it possesses more versatility in decorating than other surfaces, it is in no way as durable. It is easily scarred, broken and defaced. It is a poor choice for areas where walls may be bumped with equipment such as free weights. It is preferable in office areas or other areas where objects such as art work may be hung.

Imperial board, a type of drywall, is used in much the same way. The advantages of imperial board are that it adheres to plaster, and negates joint finishing, leaving a smoother surface. Plaster should be applied in a warm dry environment. Application in cold, damp climates will cause a bubbling effect beneath the surface, which will result in flaking.

Plaster

In the recreation facility, plaster walls will probably be found only in the racquetball/handball/wallyball court. They are almost never used today in areas where drywall can be installed. They require the services of a highly skilled craftsman. Another negative aspect is that the installation of plaster is slow, and the surface cracks and chips very easily.

Concrete

Concrete, a mixture of a cementing material and an aggregate such as gravel or sand, is a durable building material that ages very well. It can be adapted to an infinite variety of uses in engineering and architecture. An important property of concrete is its versatility. It can be formed into large monolithic structures or molded into practically any shape or form that an architect may conceive. It is inexpensive, fire proof and an excellent material for sound and heat insulation. It is strong, but lacks tensile strength, therefore it is frequently combined with steel.

The *Concrete Masonry Unit (CMU)* or concrete block, lends itself well to contemporary design. CMUs are manufactured in many shapes, sizes and textures. They are suitable for both exterior walls and interior walls in gymnasiums, swimming pools, hallways, weight rooms, locker rooms, offices, equipment issue areas and maintenance areas. Because of its versatility it is one of the more popular choices of interior wall surfaces.

Precast concrete is often used in construction of exterior walls. These slabs are preformed off site and moved on site for construction. Precast concrete slabs may be textured in a variety of ways to change their appearance. They offer an inexpensive and long-lasting construction.

Brick

Brick is also a very strong material. It lacks the versatility of concrete and is more expensive. Some feel that the beauty of brick is surpassed by no other material used in the construction of buildings. It is seldom used for load bearing wall, but rather as facing, because of its inherent warmth.

Foam core galvanized steel panels

Foam core galvanized steel panels (see photo) are a relatively inexpensive material used in the construction of walls. These panels provide an interior and exterior wall in the same unit. The foam core serves as an insulator. A disadvantage is their susceptibility to vandalism.

Melamine laminated panels

The high density melamine wall panel is becoming the most popular wall surface for racquetball/handball/wallyball and squash courts. It is stable, provides lively ball rebound, is warp resistant and provides high resistance to scrapes and abrasions. Perhaps its most attractive feature is its near maintenance-free surface.

Foam core galavanized steel panels provide an attractive exterior for recreation facilities.
(photo courtesy of Northern Illinois University)

Tile

Ceramic tile is probably the most frequently used wall surface in locker rooms and public toilets. A glazed surface, (when installed properly,) offers complete protection against water damage. Because of its versatility, the same ceramic tile can be used for floors and walls.

Plastic tile is similar to ceramic tile in appearance. It is less expensive than ceramic tile but not nearly as durable. Whereas plastic tile may be suitable for use in the home, it is not the best wall surface for public facilities.

and aids in maintenance. It is cost effective and provides much flexibility in decorating. Patterns for vinyl wallcovering should not be so deeply embossed that they hold soil or stain.

Ceilings

A ceiling is a surface of whatever shape serves to define the upper boundary of an enclosed space. It consists of an underside of the floor/roof construction, the plenum, and the ceiling membrane (figure 3-9). There are three basic types of ceiling assemblies: 1) no

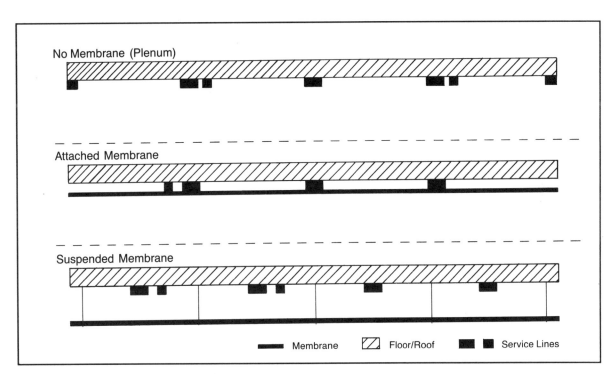

Figure 3-9: Ceiling construction

Wallcovering

Durable vinyl wallcovering is an excellent surface for walls in offices, lounge areas, and high traffic areas. A polyvinyl fluoride film will protect the covering from stains and mildew

membrane/plenum (exposed underside of the floor/roof construction; 2) attached membrane (no plenum space; membrane is attached directly to flat underside of floor/roof); and 3) suspended membrane (plenum space for mechanical systems). No membrane ceilings are often constructed in gymnasiums, while attached membrane and suspended membrane types appear in other areas of the facility. Of the suspended membrane type, acoustical tile is a common choice in rooms such as offices, activity rooms, weight/exercise rooms, etc.

Windows

Windows are an escape route for heat unless precautions are taken to install them so they are airtight. Double glazing is recommended for heat conservation (figure 3-10). The space between the panes helps to insulate. Draperies or blinds can provide additional insulation against heat loss.

Windows that open and close provide fresh air circulation during certain times of the year. Architects may argue with this suggestion, but some people prefer fresh air to artificially circulated air.

Doors

There are three major types of pedestrian entrance doors: swinging (single and double action), sliding and revolving. Swinging doors permit passage of large or small numbers but do not provide the best protection against drafts and heat loss. Sliding doors must be power-actuated if they serve as an entrance frequently used. They are not a good choice in harsher climates unless a vestibule design is used. Revolving doors will seal the outside air from the inside without the use of a vestibule. They are not a good choice for handling peak loads and are not handicap accessible.

Doors opening to the outside of a building should be durable, resistant to all weather conditions and designed to minimize heat loss from within. Heat loss can be controlled by entrance vestibules, revolving doors and weatherstripping.

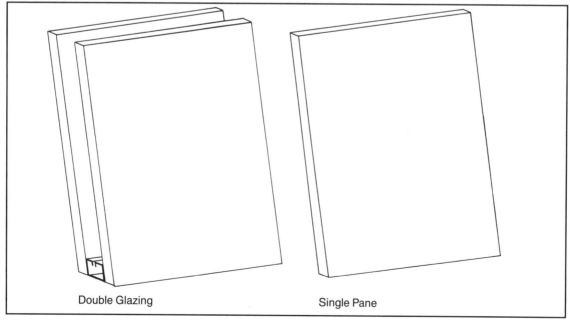

Double Glazing   Single Pane

Figure 3-10: Double glazed and single pane windows

Interior doors located in areas of high traffic or where possible impact may occur should be solid core metal-clad wood doors. Hollow core wood doors are easily broken and warped. Hollow core metal doors are easily dented.

Doors between high traffic areas should have a small window at eye level. This will prevent pedestrian collisions.

Conclusion

Selection of proper surfaces may be one of the most important exercises in the pre-design phase of construction or renovation. Technology is providing more and more innovative choices from which to choose. The choices made should be determined by the initial cost, playability, the durability of the product, and maintenance costs. No single surface satisfies all needs, but some are definitely superior to others. The most important factor in choosing is the selection of surfaces that best serve the needs of the individual situation.

Selected Bibliography

Ball, V. (1982). *The art of interior design.* New York: John Wiley and Sons.

Better homes and gardens complete guide to home repairs, maintenance, and improvements. (1980). Des Moines: Meredith Corporation.

Hand, J. (1985). *Walls, floors, and ceilings.* New York: Book Division, Times Mirror Magazine, Inc.

Here is the latest information in athletic surfaces outdoor and indoor. (1978, November). *Athletic Business,*, 11 p.24.

Klumpp, R. (1974, January). Synthetic surfacing, *Scholastic coach,* p.62.

Maintenance tips for indoor sports surfaces. (1973, May). *Athletic Business,* 5 p.30.

Picking the right floor. (1972, September) *American school and university,* p.45.

Richie, D. (1985, July/August). Aerobic dance floors. *Dance Exercise Today,* p.30.

Soft surface flooring for the entire fitness market. Cedar Rapids: Unviersal Distributions.

Special report: sports surfaces. (1982, November). *Athletic Business,* 11 p.44.

Weidhaas, E. (1979). *Architectural drafting and design.* Boston: Allyn and Bacon, Inc.

What's new in sports surfaces? (1985, November). *Athletic Business,* 11 , p.52.

Manufacturers and Distributors

AGA Hard Maple Flooring Systems
P.O. Box 246
Amasa, MI 49903

Alpha Floors, Inc.
875 N. Lively Blvd.
Wood Dale, IL 60191

Fiberesin Industries
Oconomowoc, WI 53066

World Courts, Inc.
Weymouth, MA 02169

Best Flooring Gymnasiums Tile
Mitchell Rubber Products
491 Wilson Way
City of Industry, CA 91744

Chemturf
Cpr Industries, Inc.
1801 CNA Towers
Orlando, FL 32801

Dex-O-Tex
Corssfield Products Corporation
3000 E. Harcourt
Compton, CA 90221

Dri-Dek- Self Draining Interlocking Floor Tile
Kendall Plastics
Kendall, IN. 46725

Duragrid Interlocking Safety Tiles
840 W. 2550 S.
Salt Lake City, UT 84119

Durathon
Robbins, Inc.
P.O. Box 43238
Cincinnati, OH 45244

Interlok Rubber Floor Systems
Pawling Corporation
157 Charles Colman Blvd.
Pawling, NY 12564

Mondo
Mondo U.S. A. Inc.
3313 Garden Brook Drive
Dallas, TX 75234

Proturf
Pitzer Incorporated
P.O. Box 1174
Pittsburgh, KS 66762

Sport-Flor
Sports Floor, Inc.
P.O. Box 1488
Cartersville, GA 30120

Taraflex
Gerland Industries, Inc.
10777 Westheimer, Suite 950
Houston,TX 77042

Tuflex
Tuflex Rubber Products, Inc.
4521 W. Crest Ave.
Tampa,FL 33614

Curtainwall
E.G. Smith Construction Products,Inc.
100 Walls Street
Pittsburgh, PA 15202

Thybony Wallcovering
3720 N. Kedzie Ave.
Chicago, IL 60618

Stark Ceramics,Inc.
P.O. Box 8880
Canton, OH 44711

Eckel Industries
Eckoustics Division
155 Fawcett St.
Cambridge, MA 02138

Dryotech Indistries (Glasbord)
P.O. Box 2429
Joliet, IL 60434

Boltwall
Wallcovering Division
401 Hackensack Ave.
Hackensack, NJ 07601

National Concrete Masonry Association
P.O. Box 781
Herndorn, VA 22070

Acousta-Wal
Trenwyth Acoustical Products
P.O. Box 438
Emigsville, PA 17318

4

Lighting

Lighting is probably the most important form of energy we encounter. Inefficient lighting wastes energy and money, therefore in the construction or renovation of a recreation and fitness/wellness facilities choosing the right type of lighting for each area is of utmost importance. Good artificial lighting begins with the right kind of lamp. In this chapter three types will be discussed- the incandescent, the fluorescent, and the high intensity discharge (HID) (figure 4-1).

The distribution of light in a given area will influence the type of activity conducted within it. The three basic types: direct, indirect and diffused will also be discussed.

In addition to types of lamps and presentation of light, certain planning variables and maintenance will also be addressed.

Planning Variables

The quality and quantity of light are generally the most important factors to consider when designing lighting for facilities. Several other planning variables should be considered: the intended use (the type of activity to be conducted in the area, the quality or accuracy required for the task, and the motivation of the occupant); environmental definition (the color of the reflective surfaces); and the economics of the lighting source (initial costs including installation, operational costs and maintenance).

Lamps

Incandescent

The incandescent or tungsten-filament light provides warm color quality and high adaptability and is a good choice if a bright focus is desired but it is the least energy efficient type. It is a hot light and most of the energy it produces eventually burns up the filament. The initial cost is less than other types, but in the long run, incandescent lighting is more expensive. These lights are best used in lamps as decorative fixtures in offices or in lounge areas.

Fluorescent

Unlike the incandescent bulb, the flourescent does not work on the principle of heating a wire and therefore radiates less heat. It uses up to five times less electricity than a tungsten bulb to provide the same amount of light. The fluorescent bulb provides uniformity of illumination over a large area and is an excellent source of high levels of illumination. It has a longer life which is determined by the number of times it is started and not the length of time it runs. Although it is much more efficient than the incandescent bulb, it does not allow the flexibility or produce the warm cozy quality. Fluorescent lights may produce a humming sound or may flicker if installed

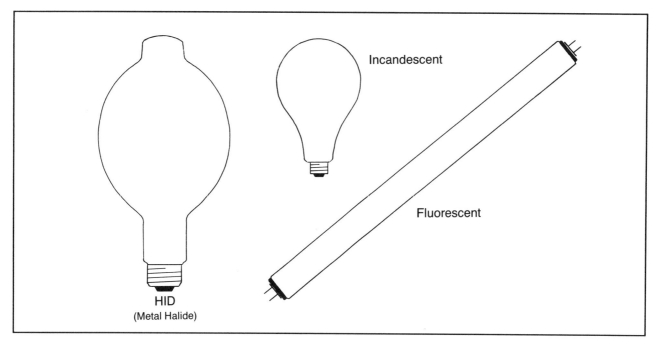

Figure 4-1 Light Sources

improperly, but these problems are usually correctable. Fluorescent lighting is good task lighting and excellent for offices, leisure crafts areas, hallways, etc. It is also an excellent source for supplementing natural light.

High Intensity Discharge

Mercury, metal halide, and sodium-vapor lights are collectively known as high intensity discharge (HID) lights and combine qualities of both the incandescent and the fluorescent light. Although they operate much like a fluorescent bulb they can be aimed much like an incandescent bulb. The result is a brilliant light that is also economical. HID lights are slow to start, however, and may take 5 to 10 minutes to reach their optimum brightness. *Metal halide* lights have a life of 6,000 to 10,000 hours. Warm up time is approximately 3 to 7 minutes and restart time is 8 to 15 minutes. This

highly efficient light source is a preferred source for play areas, but because of its restart time, it is often combined with incandescent lighting for safety purposes.

The *sodium vapor* light is six times more efficient than the incandescent light and is the most economical in operating cost. It has a life of 15,000 to 20,000 hours. A period of 3 to 4 minutes is required for warm up, and 30 to 60 seconds for restarting. It produces a color similar to that of a street light. Combining these with the metal halide can cool the color. Where great amounts of light are needed, the sodium vapor light is definitely the most economical.

Mercury vapor lights are one-third less efficient than metal halide. They have a life of 24,000 hours, a warm up time of 3 to 7 minutes, and a restart time of 3 to 6 minutes. Their light may distort color somewhat.

Presentation of Light

Mounting of light fixtures is as important as choosing the best bulb for the situation. Whereas electrical engineers can determine the location, the user must consider ceiling heights, activities to be conducted in certain areas, the appropriateness of direct versus indirect lighting, and maintenance.

Direct lighting (down lighting) from high mounted fixtures is satisfactory for activities where critical vision is not necessary when looking upwards, but is not adequate for activities that require looking upward to follow the flight of projectiles. Ceiling mounted lamps must be properly spaced to provide even distribution. The spacing of lamps should provide a slight overlap of distribution of light to minimize uneven illumination. If sources are placed too close together, a scalloping effect may occur.

In order to provide good illumination without glare, indirect lighting (light reflected from ceilings and walls) provides the best source for activities such as volleyball, badminton, tennis and other racket sports. In all cases care must be taken to ensure adequate overhead space. Indirect lighting systems rely on highly reflective surfaces for effectiveness.

Maintenance

The maintenance of any lighting system is critical to its efficiency and effectiveness as a source of illumination. Maintenance should be scheduled regularly and should include relamping, cleaning of lamps, and inspection of auxiliary units.

Relamping should be scheduled on a regular basis. Group relamping is a more efficient use of labor. Each fixture should be relamped with the proper type and wattage of lamp. Fluorescent lamp color should remain consistent with other fixtures in the area. The visual effect of multiple lamp color is undesirable.

If lamps are not properly cleaned, output will decline. The accumulation of dust an dirt will depend on the activity conducted in the area and the general maintenance of the area. Cleaning of room surfaces will also affect the reflected light from the environment.

Auxiliary units should be inspected periodically. These include ballasts, starters and other controls.

Natural lighting

Contemporary buildings are designed to make the best use of natural light. In the northern hemisphere, large windows and skylights should be oriented to the south or southeast. This will contribute to temperature conditioning due to solar gain as well as to lighting.

Lighting from windows or skylights can be a good source of illumination for some areas but for others can cause problems. Natural light in gymnasiums may cause glare and blind spots for the participant. If reflected from the water's surface in an indoor swimming pool, it can create safety hazards. Translucent glass is an excellent means of diffusing light.

Skylights should be properly designed to resist high winds at roof level. If they are not created to withstand the wind and other elements, they may leak and become a major maintenance problem.

The view into and out of the building should be considered when including skylights in the design. Overhanging trees, adjacent buildings and street lights are examples of obstacles interfering with the aesthetics of skylighting.

Light provides the stimulus which helps people perform. Proper lighting in a recreation or fitness/wellness facility can greatly enhance a participant's performance, create an environment conducive to relaxation or creativity, and consequently contribute to the total wellness of the individual.

Manufacturers and Distributors

Devoe Systems
7 Paul Kohner Place
Elmwood Park, NJ 07407

Energy Reduction Systems
1522 E. Southern Ave.
Phoenix, AZ 85202

Maximum Technology
60 Industrial Way
Brisbane, CA 94005

Musco Lighting, Inc.
P.O. Box 214
Muscatine, IA 52761

Malcolite Corporation
1021 N. DuPage Avenue
Lombard, IL 60148

Lighting Requirements

Gymnasium

Basketball	100-150 foot candles
Indoor tennis	85-100 foot candles
Indoor track	85-100 foot candles

**Racquetball/
handball court**   100 foot candles

Swimming pool (indoor)

Pool deck	50 foot candles
Over pool	100-150 foot candles

**Offices,
classrooms, etc.**   100-150 foot candles

**Corridors
and stairways**   50-75 foot candles

**Locker rooms and
showers**   50-75 foot candles

(Source: Bronzan, R.T. New concepts in planning and funding athletic, physical education and recreation, 1974.)

Selected Bibliography

Better home and gardens complete guide to home repair maintenance and improvement. (1980) Des Moines, IA: Meredith Corporation.

Bronzan, R. (1974). *New concepts in planning and funding athletic, physical education, and recreation facilities.* St. Paul: Phoenix Intermedia.

Egan, M. (1983) *Concepts in architectural lighting.* New York: McGraw Hill.

Hopkinson, R. & Kay, J. (1969) *The lighting of buildings.* New York: Frederucj A. Praeger.

Penman, K. (1977). *Planning physical education and athletic facilities in schools.* New York: John Wiley & Sons.

Planning facilities for athletics, physical education, and recreation. (1974) Athletic Institute and American Association for Health, Physical Education and Recreation.

Sudjic, D. (1985). *The lighting book.* New York: Crown, Inc.

Twice the light at half the energy. (1974, September) *American School and University,* pp.71.

5

Gymnasiums

In all probability the gymnasium is the largest and most versatile room in the recreation facility. In designing this space, every effort should be made to create a multi-use area that will accommodate a variety of activities. Care must be taken, however, to avoid creating a watered-down facility that serves no single purpose well.

In planning a large multi-purpose area consideration must be given to flooring, walls and ceilings, lighting, storage, supervisory areas, floor markings and traffic areas, and other details such as partitions, water fountains, etc. These concerns are inherent to all facilities, but choices are determined by the situation. The purpose of this chapter is to offer suggestions for selection of surfaces and accessories for the gymnasium.

Flooring

Choice of flooring may be the most important consideration facing the planning committee. Attention must be given to initial cost, maintenance, durability and playability. One can assume that the amount of money budgeted for flooring will be determined by someone other than the user. This factor may pose some limitations in selection, but the person(s) responsible for planning programs in this area should have a voice in deciding what type is chosen. It is important to have convincing evidence available for this argument. If available funds eliminate certain types of flooring, the remaining choices should be scrutinized for durability, maintenance and playability.

As mentioned in Chapter 3, no surface is perfect and everyone has a preference, based on experience or research. This author has found the use of carpeted gymnasium floors to be economical and near maintenance-free. Some controversy resulted, however, after the installation of carpeting at Northern Illinois University. Until participants were able to utilize the playing surface and evaluate its performance, it was difficult to convince them than balls do actually have a true bounce. Although wood floors remain the preference of most basketball players, carpeted floors are equally as playable and they allow much more versatility in scheduling other activities in a large multi-purpose area. For very large areas where maintenance is a concern, carpeted surfaces should not be eliminated as a viable choice.

Floor markings

It is difficult to minimize floor markings when attempting to maximize use of space. However, nothing is more confusing to the participant than a conglomeration of multi-colored lines. Care must be taken to arrange courts strategically so that this confusion will not occur. This is particularly important in the designation of tennis court and badminton court markings. See examples of court markings in figures 5-1 and 5-2.

Standards and goals

Standards for net games are sturdier and more efficient if they fit into a permanently

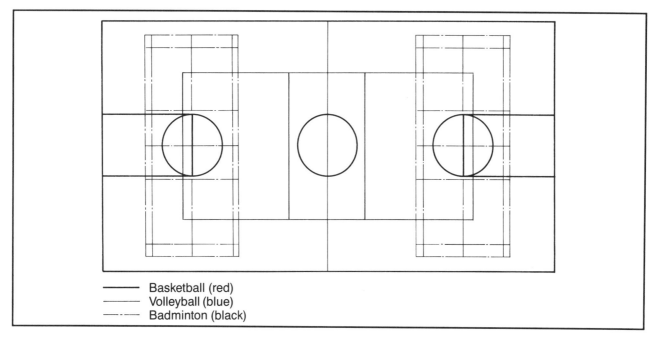

——— Basketball (red)
——— Volleyball (blue)
—·—·— Badminton (black)

Figure 5-1: Floor markings for basketball,volleyball and badminton.

In some cases, lines may be avoided altogether. For instance, basketball court boundaries may be designated by changing colors of inside court and out of bounds. The same is true for volleyball courts. This helps minimize floor markings when superimposing one court over another.

It is the management's responsibility to ensure proper court dimensions. An error made in this endeavor constitutes a costly mistake. For example, should designations for badminton or tennis standards be incorrect, nets will not fit properly and will require alterations.

recessed sleeve inside the floor. This can be accomplished regardless of choice of floor surface. A system such as this eliminates cables or other bases that pose a danger to the player. These standards are easily moved from storage to court and can be set up quickly. They are also adaptable for multiple court use.

Exposure to professional basketball through the media has introduced techniques such as the "slam dunk" to the amateur player. Consequently, manufacturers of basketball goals are busy at work designing structures that will withstand a downward force of over a thousand pounds or a goal that will break away if a downward force is exerted upon it. The additional cost of either of these is money well-spent. Constant supervision of each and every goal is impossible. Broken and bent goals will occur often if a lesser quality rim is used.

The media have likewise introduced the amateur basketball player to the glass backboard. They are more expensive but preferred by so many, that such an installation in the original project might save money in the long run.

Regardless of the type basketball goals chosen, all should be controlled by key operated electric winches. Quality cannot be stressed enough. In a multi-purpose gymnasium it is necessary to raise and lower goals several times each day. Inexpensive hardware will not last and replacement is very expensive. In gymnasiums where raising and lowering occurs rarely, manual hardware or cables operated by a hand motor may be satisfactory, but even in situations such as this, electric winches are more cost efficient.

In some situations safety standards require the installation of safety straps on all basketball goals. In any case, they are worth the initial investment to ensure the safety of the participants should a goal suddenly fall from a raised position and dislodge from ceiling supports.

Partitions

Partitions between courts in a large area allow for scheduling several different activities simultaneously. Gym divider curtains provide a mesh wall that allows breakthrough strength, visibility for supervision, and quick, easy, out of the way storage. Between-court storage is best accomplished with electrically operated fold-up curtains. These are operated by a control switch located near each curtain on the gymnasium wall. Having a control switch in close proximity to the curtain it operates allows for supervision of raising and lowering. Nets surrounding the perimeter of the play area may

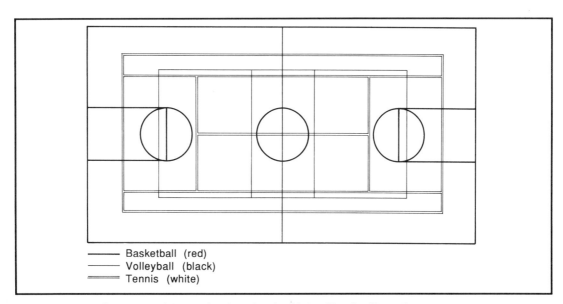

Figure 5-2: Floor markings for basketball, volleyball and tennis.

be the walk-draw type. These nets are manually operated and are easily moved into place by simply by pulling them along an overhead steel track suspended from the ceiling. Walk-draw type dividers should be stored as near a gym wall as possible. They should not unnecessarily occupy gym space.

create a potential danger for tripping.

Walls and ceilings

The concrete masonry unit (CMU) provides an excellent wall surface for the gymnasium (see Chapter 2). Providing a smooth

Key operated electric winches are a must in a multi-purpose gymnasium.
(photo: courtesy of Northern Illinois University.)

Divider curtains take a fair amount of abuse. Therefore good construction is important. Durable curtains are made of heavy vinyl mesh. Seams should be reinforced and carefully welded. An open seam will eventually lead to tearing, especially seams along the bottom of the curtain.

If curtains are not properly made and installed they can create potential safety hazards. If steel poles or chains are placed in the bottom seam of between court fold-up curtains they should not protrude outside the seam. This is a very common problem. Care should be taken to keep them out of sight at all times. Also ripped seams along the base line

surface, free of protrusions is essential. Color selection is important. While off-white provides a background that is pleasing to the eye, bright whites should be avoided. High gloss finishes are easier to maintain.

Acoustical ceiling tiles should be avoided. They will not withstand the impact of projectiles hit directly into the ceiling. If broken tiles are not replaced often, they are unsightly and create openings for balls and shuttlecocks to enter.

Lighting the gymnasium

The metal halide light is the preferred source for the gymnasium. (See Chapter 4) If used, however, it should be combined with an incandescent back-up for safety purposes.

The presentation of lighting is equally as important as the source. In areas where large projectiles are used such as volleyball and basketball, direct lighting is acceptable. However, in areas such as those used for tennis, indirect lighting provides a much more acceptable presentation.

Storage

Equipment is best stored out of sight in a separate area. The storage room should be adjacent to the gymnasium and easily accessible from an area other than an activity area. Doors should be wide enough for transportation of large pieces of equipment. Temperature and humidity control are equally as important in storage rooms as in other parts of the building. Ceilings should be high enough to accommodate large pieces of equipment. When designing storage areas, a space large enough for an increase in equipment inventory should be planned.

Supervisor's station

A glass-enclosed area adjacent to the main gymnasium is an ideal location for a supervisor's station (see photo). The area should be equipped with a desk, chair, telephone, paging system, and may also serve as a station for dispensing minimal first aid supplies. Smaller equipment used inside the gymnasium (basketballs, volleyballs, badminton and tennis equipment) may be stored and distributed in this area. Dutch doors work well as a distribution counter.

The supervisor's station should have a clear view of the gymnasium.
(Southeast Mo. State Univ., Student Rec. Center, courtesy Hastings & Chivetta Architects, Inc.)

Water fountains and cuspidors

Water fountains and cuspidors should be located side by side inside the gymnasium. The inclusion of a cuspidor will discourage participants from expectorating in water fountains. These are best located near an exit and away from the main activity area. When choosing a site for these fixtures, consideration should be given to the potential maintenance problems on floors surrounding the area. These fixtures should be recessed and flush with the wall.

Bulletin boards

Enclosed bulletin boards should be located near an exit and outside activity areas. Locking capabilities will give management control of what is posted and also prevent theft of materials. For details on bulletin boards see chapter 15.

Windows

Direct light from windows will affect performance and may create a safety hazard. Therefore, windows in a gymnasium are undesirable and should be avoided for this reason. If they are included, translucent glass will eliminate glare.

Doors

Inside doors should open away from activity areas and should have a safety glass window panel so that those entering and leaving the area can see oncoming traffic. In cases where fire doors are required and will be kept closed at all times, safety glass windows are essential. These safety glass panels should be located in the top one third of the door at eye level. Doors should be wide enough so large pieces of equipment can be transported into and out of the area.

Doors leading to the outside should fit tightly. In areas where climates are cold, small openings can create drafts that are a nuisance to the participant and the management. Openings around door facings also allow moisture to seep in causing damage to flooring. Upon completion of construction, all doors should be checked for proper fit.

Emergency exit signs should appear above all doors leading to the outside. These signs are battery operated and should be checked regularly.

Electrical outlets

Electrical outlets located on the walls around the perimeter of the gymnasium and also in between basketball courts will provide necessary sources for electricity. Protective covers should be considered as a safety feature especially in areas where children will be involved in activity. The placement of all receptacles will determine their potential use for cleaning purposes, use of electric timers and score boards, etc. Accommodations for a public address system and a pace clock should also be considered. All receptacles, both wall and floor installed should be flush mounted.

Climate control

Controlling temperature and humidity is an expensive financial undertaking in an area as large as a gymnasium. Climate control is not only related to the temperature and humidity or the surroundings but also to the design of the facility. Consideration of design is especially important if future alterations, eg. adding air-conditioning, are likely to occur. Investing in good heating and ventilating systems may well be the most important investment made in the construction or renovation of recreation and fitness/wellness facilities.

Acoustics

Good acoustical qualities should be considered in construction of all areas especially an area as large as a gymnasium. They are essential if the area is to be used for auditory events such as concerts, plays or public speaking. The type of flooring will determine to a large extent the acoustical quality. Wood floors in a large area will render poor acoustics if other measures are not taken to absorb sound. Carpeted gymnasiums on the other hand, will reduce the noise level considerably.

Careful planning of the gymnasium will ensure an area suitable for many activities. Selection of desirable surface and innovative features will be appreciated for many years by managers of the facility, maintenance staff and most of all, the participants.

References

Bronzan, R. (1974). *Planning and funding athletic, physical education and recreation facilities.* St. Paul: Phoenix Intermedia.

Gym construction: cut costs, not quality. (1984, July). *Athletic Business 7,* 23.

Keindienst, V. & Weston, A. (1978). *The recreational sports program; schools..colleges..communities.* Englewood Cliffs, Prentice Hall.

Penman, K. (1982, July) Planning the small to mid-size gymnasium. *Athletic Business 7,* p.18.

Pettine, A. (1983, October) Planning a gym. *JOHPER.* pp.58-62.

What's new in gym? (1987, March). *Athletic Business 3,* pp.56-74.

Manufacturers and Distributors

Sports Import Incorporated
P.O. Box 21108
Columbus, OH 43221

Steelco Gym Divider
Spiceland, IN 47385

Basketball Products International, Inc.
309 S. Cloverdale, D-9
Seattle, WA 98108

Gold Medal Recreational Products
Blue Mountain, AL 36201

Carron Net Company, Inc.
P.O. Box 177
Two Rivers, WI 54241

Schelde International
Court Systems
734 Alger Street S.E.
Grand Rapids, MI 49507

Douglas
Sports Nets and Equipment
P.O. Box 451
Bettendorf, IA 52722

6

Racquetball/
Handball Courts

Over the last ten years, racquetball has established itself as one of the most popular sports in the country. Whereas racquetball, handball and squash were once sports of the elite, today they are enjoyed by many who have access to facilities. The growing demand for court space has necessitated expanding recreation and fitness facilities to serve these enthusiasts.

In addition to accommodating racket sports, these courts can be equipped with net facilities so they may be used for wallyball, a sport growing in popularity among college and university students. The purpose of this chapter is to offer suggestions for the construction of racquetball, handball and squash courts that are durable and easy to maintain.

Design

If a single battery of courts is constructed, courts should be located side by side, sharing side walls. A double battery of courts should be separated by a corridor approximately ten feet wide which extends along the area adjacent to the back walls (see figure 6-1). Observation areas may be built at least twelve feet above the court floor and follow a corridor extending above the one separating the courts. If glass enclosed courts are constructed, there is little need for an observation area above the courts. Racquetball/handball courts are 40 feet long

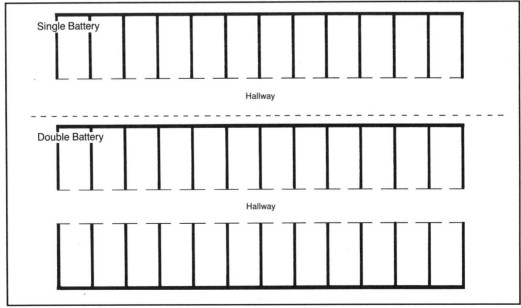

Figure 6-1: single and double battery of racquetball courts.

and 20 feet wide with a ceiling height of 20 feet and a backwall of at least 12 feet high.

Flooring

In selecting flooring for these courts consideration should be given to the skill level of players who will use the court, durability of the materials used in construction,   and maintenance of the courts. In almost all cases, maple flooring is far superior to any other surface. It is durable, easy to maintain, and acceptable to all skill levels.   The anchored channel system (see Chapter 3) is more resistant to high humidity and is therefore suitable for these courts.   Synthetic flooring, with a monolithic surface may be acceptable and desirable where extremely humid climates exist or where there is danger of flooding.

Walls and Ceilings

A good wall provides a consistent, even bounce, is free from dead spots, resists chipping and pitting, and is easily maintained with soap and water. They provide the same quality and playability as plaster.

The fiberglass reinforced resin plaster wall has the durability of the melamine laminate panel and the look of plaster. Its monolithic surface resists chipping and never needs painting. Like the melamine panel, it can be easily washed and restored to its original appearance with mild detergent and water.

The glass back wall provides an opportunity for viewing by spectators and instructors. Whereas glass is preferred by some players, others will choose to play in a solid wall court. Therefore inclusion of both types within a facility is desirable. Glass back walls are expensive and will increase maintenance time slightly.

Ceilings in these courts must withstand the impact of wallyballs as well as racquetballs, handballs, and squash balls. Acoustical tiles will reduce the noise level but will not withstand the contact made by balls hit hard against the ceiling.   In a melamine panel system a continuation of the same panel will provide a near vandal-proof ceiling. It is a good tradeoff for an echo. The same applies in the fiberglass resin plaster system.   A continuation of the same material provides a more durable ceiling.

Doors

Doors should be solid core with a flush fitted observation window and a flush pull on the court side of the door. They should open and close easily and fit properly, providing a uniform surface on the court side. If a lock and key system is required for security, it should be installed separately from the pull latch. Systems that function separately are not inclined to malfunction simultaneously.

The height of the door should be also studied. Doors shorter than five feet are an inconvenience to the participant and are often a maintenance problem.   Doors with low clearance may inhibit the use of certain types of scaffolding or machinery used to service ceiling fixtures.

Providing a means of storage for small items, either inside the court wall or the door is desirable. Otherwise participants will either place keys, wallets, jewelry, etc. inside the playing area in a corner, creating a dangerous situation, or outside the court. Belongings left outside the court create clutter an encourage theft.

Lighting

Metal halide lights offer good lumination and are relatively inexpensive to operate. The only drawback is their delayed starting time. After being turned off they will not reach full lumination again for approximately five minutes. This may be a problem if court use is controlled by lights being turned on and off. If participants are required to claim court reservations five minutes prior to playing time, this may not be a problem.

Fluorescent lamps are more economical to operate, require no warm up time, are less expensive to replace and emit less heat than metal halide lights. Many experts argue, however, that they do not produce the quality of light that metal halides produce.

Light fixtures should be recessed in the ceiling and protected with a non-breakable cover. These covers should be anchored securely so that they will not dislodge under impact.

Control of court use may be accommodated by various methods of light control. These include lights that are activated with the opening and closing of court doors, or an annunciator panel or signal board controlled by an attendant and located at an access point where players are likely to check in.

Temperature and ventilation

Because of the strenuous nature of racquetball, handball and squash, courts should be relatively cool (65 degrees). Good ventilation is essential when participants perspire within a small area. Air conditioning the courts will address both these concerns.

Squash court variations

Squash courts differ in dimension from the handball/racquetball court. A singles squash court is 32 feet long and 18 1/2 feet wide with a ceiling height of 16 feet. A doubles court is 45 feet long and 25 feet wide with a ceiling height of 20 feet. Squash also requires a one inch metal strip, 17 inches wide on the front wall. Other rule modifications will have to be made since racquetball/handball courts do not have side wall markings for squash.

The number of squash courts should be determined by the interest shown by participants in the area. Unless there is a great demand, construction of courts exclusively for squash is not a good investment.

Manufacturers continue to introduce new and innovative materials used in the construction of court systems and the interest in individual racket sports continues to grow. Racquetball, handball, squash and more recently wallyball are being enjoyed by individuals of all ages. These courts should be included in the construction or renovation of all recreation or fitness/wellness facilities.

Selected Bibliography

Penman, K. (1979, May) Construction and maintenance of racquetball courts. *Athletic Purchasing and Facilities.* p.30.

Malloy, A. (1978) *Winning squash.* Chicago: Contemporary Books, Inc.

Manufacturers and Distributors

Fiberesin Industries
Oconomoc, WI 53066

Intracor
Sports Surfacing Division
P.O. Box 1948
Lake Oswego, OR 97035

Strongwall Systems, Inc.
P.O. 201
Ridgewood, NJ 07451

Tectum, Inc.
105 S. Sixth Street
P.O. Box 920
Newark, OH 43055

The Court Company
2876 Putting Green
Memphis, TN 38115

W & W Glass Products LTD
300 Airport Executive Park
Spring Valley, NY 10977

World Court, Inc.
Weymouth, MA 02169

7 Weight/ Exercise Room

It's safe to say that no other area in the recreation or fitness/wellness facility will receive more use and abuse than the weight-exercise room. Therefore, it is of utmost importance that design and construction of this facility be carefully considered. The purpose of this chapter is to give the reader ideas regarding design and construction of this area. Suggestions pertaining to equipment will also be made.

Size and location

Size is a critical factor. A minimum of 2500 square feet of space should be planned for any recreation or fitness/wellness facility. For large institutions, 5000 square feet may or may not be adequate. It seems that no matter how much space is devoted to this area, its popularity will soon deem it too small. Important factors to consider in determining size are the type of equipment housed in the area, the number of activities conducted within the space, an area for warm up and cool down, and an area for a supervisor's station.

Because of the noise factor, this room should not be located near administrative offices and other quiet areas. For the same reason, it should not be located on an upper level, unless the area below is not affected by the noise of free weights dropping to the floor.

Flooring

Flooring in weight/exercise rooms must support heavy machines and withstand the impact of free weights being dropped on it. Prefabricated rubber flooring has been a popular surface for this area; however, some rubber surfaces have a tendency to crack, especially in the free weight area. Rubber installed over concrete does not absorb the shock of dropped weights. Consequently, the equipment may crack and break on impact. Rubber is more suitable in areas where machines are housed, but in free weight areas, the addition of wooden platforms helps maintain the floor surface and the equipment. Carpeting installed over the platform helps absorb sound.

As mentioned in Chapter 3, rubber surfaces are available in rolls or tiles. Tiles create more seams than rolled goods, a fact that should be recognized when considering maintenance.

Since rubber products are difficult to clean, light colored surfaces may not be preferable. The color gold is especially difficult to clean, whereas red and brown surfaces show less soil. A salt and pepper, confetti, or chip pattern will show less dirt than solid colors. A pebble or grain surface will provide more traction than a smooth surface, therefore rubber surfaces are much preferred to monolithic, poured in place urethane surfaces.

Carpet is a suitable surface for areas where

machines are housed, as well as free weight areas. The addition of a wood platform in free weight areas will prolong the life of the equipment. Carpet is easily maintained and will reduce the noise level.

Ideally the free weights should be housed in a separate room, although lack of space may prevent this arrangement. If free weights and machines are to occupy the same room, the free weight area may be distinguished from the machine area by change in floor color or a bold line painted on the floor.

Walls and ceiling

Walls must likewise be durable. Any type of wall board is a not a good choice. Concrete masonry units (CMUs) provide the best surface for this area. They are less likely to chip if accidentally bumped with free weights, are noise resistant, and can be decorated with wall paint. A large viewing window or glass wall in the weight/exercise room will aid in supervision of the area.

Ceilings should be constructed of acoustical tile and should be a minimum of 12 feet high in areas where free weights are used. This allows ample room for tall lifters to extend weights above the head.

Mirrors

Mirrors are a must in this area. They should be installed far enough above the floor so that they will not be kicked or broken by ill placed bar bells and plates. Additional information on mirrors is included in Chapter 14.

Doors

Double doors (6 feet wide) with removable mullions will allow for transfer of large pieces of machinery to and from the area. Doors should have a window at eye level for safety of individuals entering and leaving the area.

Lighting

Fluorescent lights recessed in the ceiling provide the most cost efficient lighting for weight/exercise rooms. This lighting is adequate for tasks performed in this area. Natural light may also be utilized, however, windows should be located at least 5 feet above the floor.

Ventilation

The provision for adequate ventilation in this area cannot be stressed enough. Weight/exercise rooms are often filled to capacity, creating a room full of warm, perspiring bodies. If ventilation is not adequate, the area will become humid and body odors will linger. Those involved in planning would be well advised to inquire about the capabilities of the ventilating system. Some feel that there is no substitute for fresh air in this area. This, of course, requires installation of windows that open and close.

Equipment

Weight machines are categorized in basically two ways: weight loaded and pneumatic resistance (hydraulic canister). Weight loaded machines are more popular among weight lifters and body builders and are found more often in health clubs, wellness/fitness facilities and recreation facilities. However, machines which offer resistance by means of a hydraulic cylinder are becoming more popular among those using these facilities for general fitness.

cables, pulleys, and/or cams to be serviced and maintained.

A well equipped weight/exercise facility will include machines for exercising all major muscle groups. When the time comes to select equipment, a meeting should be arranged with representatives from several companies. Most are eager to bring a piece of equipment to you for demonstration. This is a much better means of selection than choosing from a catalog. Most of these salespersons will diagram a proposed layout based on types of machinery desired and available space. The time spent with

The weight/exercise room should include machines for all major body parts. (photo courtesy of Northern Illinois University.)

When selecting equipment, the manager of a facility should consider maintenance and upkeep on machinery. Weight loaded machines generally need more upkeep and repair than those offering resistance through a hydraulic cylinder. In the case of the latter, there is basically only one operating part, the cylinder; whereas in weight loaded machines there are

knowledgeable persons is well worth the effort. Inclusion of both weight loaded machines and hydraulic resistance machines will help satisfy all participants.

Apparatus

Other equipment which might be included

in a weight/exercise facility includes speed bags, body bags, chinning bars, and wall pulleys. If all are not mounted properly, they will soon become detached from walls or ceilings. Body bags are especially difficult to mount successfully. Including these additions to the weight/exercise facility will undoubtedly increase maintenance.

Upholstery

Upholstery on all machines will eventually need replacement. Durability depends on the weight of the fabric and the quality of the backing. Heavy vinyl with a tough backing is the best choice. It is easily cleaned and will last a respectable length of time if properly cared for. Upholstery should be cleaned daily with a mild detergent and water. Accumulation of perspiration and body oils will not only create health problems, but will cause upholstery to depreciate more quickly.

Requiring participants to wear proper attire will also prolong the life of the upholstery. Jeans or shorts made with rivets will often cause tears in the fabric.

Circuit training

Circuit training incorporates the use of machines and aerobic exercise, and provides an excellent comprehensive workout for individuals who have time constraints. This innovative approach to exercise should be investigated prior to planning the weight-exercise facility. If this concept is an option, consideration should be given to the following guidelines:

1. Use equipment that is easily adjusted. Either weight loaded equipment or pneumatic resistance equipment is suitable. Pneumatic resistance equipment, if used properly, will give the participant

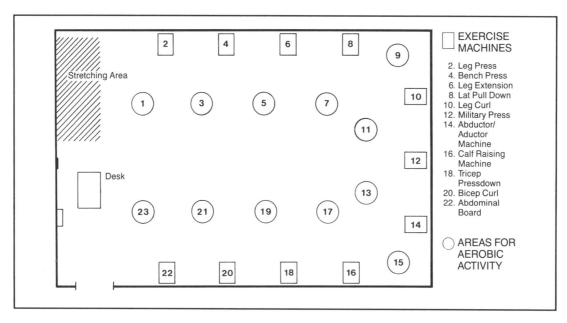

Figure 7-1: Exercise circuit

a better aerobic workout. Because of the time element, free weights should not be used.

2. Design the circuit so that the first and last stations are aerobic. (See figure 7-1) This allows the participant a brief warm up and cool down period.

3. A visual description of the exercise should be posted at each station. This helps the participant perform activities properly.

4. The circuit should be set up so that the traffic flow pattern allows ease in moving from one station to the other.

5. Approximately twelve stations are recommended. Machines should be arranged so that participants begin exercising large muscle groups, moving to smaller muscle groups. Arrangement of machines should also provide a sequence for alternating activity for upper and lower body. (See figure 7-1.)

6. A file box should be located at the supervisor's station so participants can have access to materials and personal records needed for their workout.

7. Provisions should be made for audio output. Recordings are often used for directing participants on the circuit. These recordings should tell the individual when to move from station to station.

Free weights

Free weights are a necessity for the weight lifter and the body builder, and are preferred by many individuals who use them for developing body tone. Therefore, no weight/exercise facility is complete without them. The following inventory is suggested as a complete set of free weights for a facility serving 45-50 individuals at any one time:

•Two squat racks	•One dumbell rack
•Two flat benches	•Two incline benches
•Two free benches	•Two preacher benches
•Two abdominal sit up benches	•Five olympic bars- 45 lbs.
•Three cambered bars - 25 lbs.	•Twenty two 45 lb. plates
•Six 35 lb. plates	•Five weight-plate storage racks
•Eighteen 10 lb. plates	•Sixteen 5 lb. plates
•One complete set of dumbells from 5 to 100 lbs.	•Twelve 2.5 lb. plates
	•Fourteen 25 lb .plates

Storage

Ideally, free weights should be stored on racks and away from the lifting area. A storage room adjacent to the weight/exercise room will serve this purpose.

The popularity of the weight/exercise room makes it a drawing card for many facilities. Therefore, careful planning is essential for marketing purposes as well as for providing an area that will serve large numbers of participants for an extended period of time. Planning for expansion may be the most crucial consideration in developing an area such as this.

Selected Bibliography

Hunter, E. (1984). Give a lift to your weightroom facilities.   In Vendle, B., Dutler, D., Holsberry, W., Jones, T., and Ross, M. (Eds.) *Interpretive aspects of intramural-recreational sports.* pp.191-206.

Schlobohm, A. (1988) Exercise Circuit. Unpublished.

Manufacturers and Distributors

Western Athletic Distribotors, Inc.
2420 Oakton
Arlington Heights,IL 60005

Bally Fitness Products Corporation
10 Thomas Road
Irvine, CA 92714

Universal
Box 1270
Cedar Rapids, IA 52406

Hydra Fitness Industries
2121 Industrial Blvd.
P.O. Box 599
Belton, TX 76513

Nautilus
12750 Merit Drive, Suite 516
Dallas, TX 75251

Nordic Track
PSI 124 K Columiba Ct.
Chaska, MN 55318

Tempromark International Inc.
(Bump guard rails)
206 Mosher Avenue
Woodmorg, NY 11598

8 Areas for Creative Expression

Activity Room

A multi-use room can serve many purposes. If properly designed it can accommodate creative activities such as dance as well as martial arts, and aerobic dance exercise. It can also serve as a meeting room or projection room. Aside from careful selection of flooring, wall surfaces, lighting, etc. the addition of several features will broaden the possibilities for use.

Flooring

The primary purpose of the multi-use room will be for physical activity of some sort. Therefore in selecting flooring, prime consideration should be given to the type of activities which will be conducted here and secondary consideration to meetings or other non-physical events.

The maple floor is a durable floor and will serve a variety of activities. The anchored channel system offers a resilient surface suitable for dance, aerobic exercise, and various martial arts. It wears well, so that if proper precautions are taken, occasional meetings will not damage it.

Most synthetic flooring can be used for the multi-use room. It is not nearly as attractive as wood and probably no more durable. As mentioned previously, some types are difficult to clean.

Walls and ceilings

The concrete masonry unit (CMU) provides an excellent wall surface for the multi-use activity room. Whereas drywall may be adequate for dance and aerobic exercise, it will not withstand the impact of kicks delivered by the martial arts enthusiast. As mentioned previously, the CMU can provide a durable, inexpensive, and attractive wall surface.

The inclusion of a movable partition will create an additional area for activity. Large partitions should be equipped with a key operated electrical system that allows for ease in opening and closing. Preferably, partitions should also be sound proof and at the very least, sound resistant.

Lighting

The fluorescent light provides good lumination for a multi-use room. If windows are included for utilization of natural light, they should be located high enough above the floor to ensure a safe environment for activities such as certain forms of martial arts. Natural light may not be a good choice if the activity room is to be used as a projection area.

Wall unit sound system

A wall unit stereo sound system consisting of a turn table and tape player/recorder is an ideal feature for maximizing use of space and eliminating transportation of audio equipment. This unit should be equipped with a durable lock so it can be secured when not in use.

Projection accommodations

If the multi-use area is to be used as a projection room, an electrical outlet should be installed inside the floor approximately 25 feet from the wall. Likewise, a motorized screen which can be recessed into the ceiling when not in use should be installed. Screens equipped with light-switch type controls will provide ease in operating the screen between up and down positions. Most electronically-controlled screens will have preset up and down switch limits.

Other options to consider for an activity room include cork boards and liquid chalk writing systems. These items are described in detail in Chapter 14.

Storage

Large storage closets with double door should be adjacent to the multi-use room. During the planning phase of the project, the purpose of the space should be determined. If large mats are to be stored in this area, doors must be wide enough to accommodate a mat truck. The same also applies for storage of tables and chairs which may also be stored on trucks.

Creative arts centre

According to Albert Tillman, "when we shape and mold an arts and crafts project, we put our personalty into it. We call it self-expression." The complete wellness facility will include an area where participants may engage in activity which will provide a medium for self-expression and creativity.

Wood is an attractive and durable floor surface for an activity room.
(photo courtesty of Krannert Center, Champaign, IL.)

Creative arts centres may be as simple as a large room equipped with tables and chairs, good lighting and a sink. It may include equipment and facilities for woodworking, ceramics, jewelry crafts, weaving, silk screening, photography and other crafts. A well-rounded area will likely include all of the above. The purpose of this chapter is to offer suggestions for design of a creative arts centre which includes facilities for these activities and others. Recommendations for surfaces as well as equipment will be made.

Flooring

Maintenance is a big factor in selecting a floor surface for this area. Vinyl tile or concrete are best in areas where spills frequently occur. If concrete is selected, it should be sealed.

In woodworking areas, vinyl and concrete may become slippery with an accumulation of sawdust, therefore some type of open grid or platform may be placed in front of machinery. This will allow sawdust particles to fall through the openings. These platforms should not be more than an inch or two from the floor. Rubber or vinyl mats are suggested.

Walls and ceilings

Walls made of gypsum board or CMUs are adequate for this area. Use of high gloss paint on either will make maintenance easier. Ceilings should be at least 12 feet high, and may be constructed of acoustical tile or gypsum board.

Doors

Doors should be wide enough so large pieces of equipment and large projects can be moved into and out of the area. Creative arts centres should also be located near freight delivery docks with a door possibly opening onto this area for convenience in delivering supplies.

Lighting

A combination of fluorescent lighting and natural lighting provide good illumination for a creative arts centre. Fixtures should be recessed inside the ceiling to prevent damage to them should large objects come in contact with the ceiling. Windows which open and close will provide natural light and will provide fresh air in areas where ventilation is important.

Plumbing

A sink is a must in an all purpose area where "wet" crafts occur. Special plumbing is needed in a photography lab. Sinks should be equipped with a trap to prevent debris from clogging the drain. Soap and paper towel dispensers should be located above sinks.

Electricity

Power machinery and kilns may have special electrical requirements. This must be determined at the time when the area is being designed. Failure to plan ahead will mean additional electrical services prior to use of equipment.

Electrical outlets for hand tools and such should be located on the wall above counter top work surfaces. Electrical outlets for use of tools and equipment at table top workbench stations should be suspended from a ceiling mounted outlet. Floor outlets should not be installed in an area where sawdust and other types of debris can become trapped inside them. Floor outlets often create a safety hazard for pedestrian traffic.

An emergency switch which "cuts" all electrical current in an area where power machinery is being used, should be located on a wall in a conspicuous place. This is a required safety feature.

Ventilating and exhaust

Good ventilating systems are essential to the health and safety of persons using this area. There are two types: dilution and local exhaust. Dilution systems bring in outside air to dilute "bad" air. Local exhaust systems capture "bad" air at the source and route it outside before it has a chance to mix with inside air. Both types of systems are needed.

Storage

Storage should be provided for safe keeping of tools, projects and chemicals. Tools and projects can be stored in lockers or cabinets with locking capabilities. Cabinets and drawers where tools are stored may be labeled with tags indicating content. A simple plexiglass plate will provide this option.

Chemicals may require a special type of fire-safe cabinet. As with any area, built-in cabinetry will provide the best use of space, both for storage and counter-top usage.

Safety equipment and supplies

Safety equipment and supplies for all areas of a creative arts centre include items such as extinguishers, an eye wash, and charts with

safety regulations. All these items should be located in a conspicuous place. Local fire departments should have some input into selection of cabinets for storage and for selection of fire extinguishers.

Equipment for special areas

The following equipment is suggested for special areas of a creative arts centre:

Multi-purpose area
- Heavy wooden tables
- Adjustable stools
- Cabinets and storage lockers

Woodworking shop
- Table saw
- Radial arm saw
- Jig saw
- Power sander
- Joiner/planer
- Drill press
- Lathe
- Large workbench tables/vises
- Storage cabinets

Photography Darkroom and Processing Lab
- Enlargers

Ceramics Facility
- Kilns
- Potter's wheels
- Dry/Wet cabinets
- Clay storage bins

A Creative Arts Centre can begin as a simple facility and expand to include much more sophisticated tools and equipment. Because of its uniqueness it may take time and patience to develop programs in this area, but eventually managers of recreation and fitness/wellness facilities will realize its benefits.

Because of the range of information necessary to design and organize a facility such as this, an attempt has been made simply to introduce the concept and the basics of design.

Selected Bibliography

Better Homes and Gardens Books. (1976), *Treasures from throwaways.* Meredith Corporation.

Black, M. (1980), *The key to weaving.* New York: MacMillan Publishing Co., Inc.

Bohm, H. (1971), *Making simple constructions.* London: Studio Vista Limited.

Carey, M. (1972). *Candlemaking.* New York: Golden Book.

Deyrup, A. (1971), *Getting started in batik.* London: Collier MacMillan Publishers.

Epple, A. (1974), *Nature crafts.* Radnor,PA: chilton Book Company.

Fischman, W. (1978), *Furniture finishing.* Indianapolis: Babbs-Merrill.

Harper, W. (1973), *Step by step enameling.* New York: Golden Book.

Herr, G. (1975), *Carving collectables.* Danville, IL: Herr Publications.

Isenberg, A. & Isenberg, S. (1983), *How to work in stained glass.* Radnor, PA: Chilton Book Company.

Johnson, J. (1975), *Discovery book of crafts.* New York: Vineyard Books, Inc.

Lindbeck, J. Duenk, L. & Hansen, M. (1969), *Basic crafts.* Peoria, IL: Chas, A. Bennett Co., Inc.

Loeb, J. (1975), *The leather book.* A & W Visual Li brary.

McCann, M. (1985), *Health hazards manual for artists.* New York: Nick Lyons Books.

Moran, J. (1979), *Leisure activities for the mature adult.* Minneapolis: Burgess Publishing Company.

Nadler, B. (1978), *The color printing manual.* Garden City,NY: American Photographic Book Publishing Co., Inc.

Newman, T. (1976), *Woodcraft, basic concepts and skills.* Radnor, P: Chilton Book Co.

Plummer, B. (1974). *Earth presents, how to make beautiful gifts from nature's beauty.* A & W Visual Library.

Schottle, H. (1979), *Color photography: the portrait.* Garden City, NY: American Photography Book Publishing Company, Inc.

The beautiful crafts book. (1978), New York: Sterling Publishing Company.

The Kodak library of creative photography. (1985), Time -Life Books.

Wagner, W. (1980), Modern woodworking. South Holland, IL: The Goodheart-Willcox Company, Inc.

Waller, J. (1985), *Safe practices in the arts and crafts, a studio guide.* New York: College Arts Association of America.

Wardell, R. & Wardell, J. (1985), *Introduction to stained glass, a teaching manual.* Ontario: Wardell Publications.

Weiskopf, D. (1975), *A guide to recreation and leisure.* Boston: Allyn and Bacon, Inc.

Manufacturers and Distributors

Vans Art Supply
1290 N W. Highway
Des Plaines, IL 60016

Brodhead Garrett Co.
4560 E. 71st Street
Cleveland, OH 44105

Rio Grande Albuquerque
6901 Washington N E
Albuquerque, NM 87109

Satco Division of Satterlee
(Woodworking Equipment)
924 S. 19th Avenue
Minneapolis, MN 55404

Vega Enterprises
(Woodworking Equipment)
RR # 2 Box 193
Decatur, IL 62526

Barricks Manufacturing Company
(Folding Tables)
P.O. Box 1612
Gadsden, AL 35902

9

Swimming Pools

The design and construction of a swimming pool is a project of great magnitude and should never be attempted without the expertise of an experienced pool consultant. The purpose of this chapter is to provide basic information regarding design, filtration, chemical treatment, lighting, deck equipment and innovative features of pool design. Specifications are in most cases determined by state codes. Therefore, those involved in design and construction of pools should be aware of these specifications and restrictions. A list of references is included at the end of this chapter for more specific information and guidelines.

Design

Whereas it may seem impossible to design a swimming pool that will meet all program needs, the ultimate goal is diversity. Diversity leads to greater income potential and may help to pay for the operation. In designing pools, four aquatic uses should be considered: competitive swimming, instructional swimming, recreational swimming, and swimming for fitness.

Competitive

When designing competitive pools, consideration should be given to the level of competition, specifications of the governing bodies for competitive swimming and diving and whether or not the pool will ever be used for other purposes. Pools designed with only competitive events in mind may not be suitable for recreational and educational purposes. The rules of most competitive bodies call for a minimum of depth of 4 feet, which would not be suitable for conducting instruction or for recreational use by children. At the writing of this book, the ruling bodies for competitive events in the United States are the National Federation of State High School Associations; the National Collegiate Athletic Association; United States Swimming, Inc.; United States Diving, Inc.; United States Water Polo; and United States Synchronized Swimming. For international competition, the Federation Internationale de Natation Amateur is the ruling body.

Instructional

Requirements for instructional pools include provisions for teaching stations (eg. float lines for separating skill levels), a warm water section (86-92 degrees F), underwater lights, provisions for underwater sound, ample deck space for teaching purposes, a classroom adjacent to the pool deck and adequate storage space. The most important consideration should be the availability of shallow water space.

Depths of instructional pools depend on the age of the participant. Junior pools serving preschool children vary in depth from 6 inches to 20 inches for toddlers and 24 inches to 48 inches for ages 4 to 6 years. For adult swimmers, depths can range from 3 1/2 feet to 6 feet. Various means of altering pool depths for instructional purposes are covered in the section of the chapter on innovative design features. Pool bottoms should be gradually and uniformly pitched. An expert pool consultant can direct the designers to state codes which determine the level of pitch to the pool.

Recreational pools will probably include diving boards and/or platforms. The height of the boards and platforms is determined by state codes. The designer should also consult the National Swimming Pool Foundation Design Compendium for specifications.

Fitness activities conducted in a swimming pool might include water aerobics as well as lap swimming. Water aerobics would require a large area of shallow water while lap swimming will probably require lane markers.

Lane markers are essential for competitive swimming.
(photo: Simon Center, St. Louis, courtesy of Hastings & Chivetta Architects, Inc.)

Recreational and fitness

Designs for pool used for recreational purposes and for fitness activities are greatly affected by the diversity among users. Research has shown that pools designed primarily for recreational purposes should have at least 80 percent shallow area (less than 5 ft. deep).

Finishes

Pool finishes include protective coatings, tile, plaster, and integral finishes. Protective coatings are the most diverse. Rubber-based paints are inexpensive and are adequate for short term protection. While initially inexpensive, they can be very expensive to recoat. Therefore there should be greater sensibility on the preventative maintenance. Maintenance personnel should be taught to maintain these coatings and be particularly sensitive to water chemistry. Improper water chemistry can actually deteriorate rubber-based paints. If constant recoating is necessary, the surface will eventually break down and require major repairs. Proper application of coatings and proper long-term maintenance will determine the longevity of the coating. In addition to rubber, other coatings include neoprene rubber, polyvinyl chloride, polysulphide, polyisoprene, and polyurethane.

Tile finishes are more permanent than the protective coating. However, cost often prohibits its use. It is often used solely on the water line band portion of the pool. This allows easy maintenance of the scum line that forms around the rim of the pool.

Plaster finishes provide a durable surface which will last as long as ten years, and are less expensive than tile. Selection of plaster or any other pool surface, will depend on whether or not it is located indoors or outdoors. If it is an outdoor pool, its geographic location will play a part in this decision. Care should be taken not to use cleaning chemicals with a high acid content. This will shorten the life of the finish.

A dead white color should be used for the pool shell in both indoor and outdoor pools. Dark colors should be avoided for safety reasons. Most states require light colored shells. Before determining color, the designer should refer to state codes.

Circulation and filtration

Circulation and filtration are technical processes which give a crystal clear appearance to water. These processes, though very technical, have been somewhat simplified for the pool manager by computerization of mechanical equipment.

The rate of exchange of pool water is determined by local health agencies. Rate of exchange is based on water volume and usage. Pumps should run continuously for proper filtration to occur.

Allowing for displacement of water is important in competitive pools. Surge tanks provide a means for regulating this displacement so that continuous skimming action occurs. They are very expensive and probably need not be considered for pools used for anything other than competition.

Perimeter overflow systems are used for skimming the water and removing surface film. Techniques include recessed and partially recessed methods, rimflow construction, rollout and surface skimmers. Whichever system is utilized, it should extend around the perimeter or a portion of it. It is likewise important to ensure when the pool is installed that it is level, allowing consistent flow of water when the pool is not in use.

Water supply inlets may be placed either in the pool floor or in the side walls. In large pools, floor inlets are recommended for greater dispersement of clean water coming from the filter.

At least one main outlet should be placed

inside the pool floor at the deepest location. Depending on the size of the pool, multiple drains are preferable, each placed approximately 8 to 10 feet from the side walls and outside the diving area. They must be covered with protective grates that pose no danger to swimmers.

Chemical treatment

Chlorine is the most widely used chemical for disinfecting pool water. It is utilized in one of three states: chlorine gas, calcium hypochloride (solid), and sodium hypochlorite (liquid). Chlorine is the gaseous form is the least expensive. However, the initial cost of systems installation is expensive. It is dangerous when it is not handled properly. Additional safety precautions must be taken in storage of tanks. Maintenance staff should be carefully trained to handle chlorine gas.

Calcium hypochlorite is manufactured in granular and tablet form. This solid form has a limited shelf life and may be flammable.

Sodium hypochlorite does not require mixing as does the solid form, and creates little danger in storage if well ventilated. Its shelf life is very short (2 to 3 months) and it is more expensive than the solid form.

In the overall analysis, gas chlorine is the most efficient means of chemically treating a pool. Whichever method of treatment is selected, the pool manager must consider that staffing for maintenance is the key to protecting the overall investment.

Several considerations are important when selecting the kind of chemical treatment

to be used, including the price, the geographic location and the ease of delivery , the staff responsible for maintaining the pool and whether or not automation and computerization are a part of the plan.

Pool lighting

Natural

When natural lighting is utilized, it must be carefully incorporated into the design. Considerations should include the possible safety problems of glare and energy loss through the glass.

Certain design features can eliminate these problems. The position of the glass opening will determine whether or not direct sunlight enters the pool area causing glare. Multiple-glazing of glass panels will help prevent energy loss and can enhance passive solar qualities with southern exposure.

Natural lighting can enhance the quality of the pool by bringing the outside environment inside, thus eliminating the boxed-in feeling. This makes the pool much more attractive and conducive to use, which may be a factor in generating revenue.

Artificial

Lighting for indoor pools may be provided by metal halide, mercury vapor or fluorescent bulbs. For details regarding illuminations see Chapter 1. For all types of lighting, a practical system of maintenance should be considered. Provisions for replacement of bulbs located over the pool surface should be incorporated in the design, choices include the selection of fixtures that are equipped with devices which allow raising and lowering, or with scaffolding or other structural means for reaching fixtures. Reference should be made to state codes determining lighting regulations.

Temperature and humidity control

Pool designers should have a complete understanding of the principles of condensation and relative humidity. The control of temperature and humidity are critical to the comfort of the swimmer and to marketing the pool. Swimmers are much more inclined to choose a comfortable environment than a pool where walls are sweating and a strong smell of chlorine hangs in the air.

Providing adequate temperature and humidity control likewise protect the investment and is critical to energy conservation. Condensation build-up can cause deterioration of walls and ceilings and create an environment that is unattractive and often unsafe for the participant. Energy can be conserved if in designing the facility, consideration is given to certain factors. The effects of daily temperature variations, outside humidity, year round variations of temperature, availability of sunlight, and windspeed on the conditions within the facility are ways to conserve energy. Proper insulation and orientation significantly influence energy conservation as well.

Deck equipment

Selection of deck equipment depends primarily on the type of pool being designed and its potential use. Competitive pools need provisions for starting platforms, while pools used for recreational purposes will probably include slides. All pools require safety equipment. Persons involved in swimming pool design should visit other pools and see what they have in the way of deck equipment. A shopping list can result from such a visit.

Starting platforms

If pools are to be used for competition and starting platforms are needed, those responsible for design should consult the National Swimming Pool Foundation Compendium for Design for specifications. State codes regulate size, distance above water, depth of water, etc. With the rise in litigation, consideration may be given to portable clocks which can be removed between competitive events when pools may be used for other swimming activities. This will prevent persons who do not know how to use them from sustaining possible injury.

Lifeguard chairs

Lifeguard chairs can be movable or permanently installed into the pool deck. The advantage of movable chairs is that they can be moved off the deck so the area can be used for other purposes. A disadvantage is that swimmers become accustomed to the location and will look to that spot for help should the services of a lifeguard be needed. If chairs are moved around, swimmers may become confused.

The seat on either type of chair should be comfortable to sit in, and swivel so that guards can turn from side to side with ease. Seats heights are determined by state codes. Most lifeguard chairs are mounted on a platform so the guard can stand. All are equipped with ladders either on the back of the stand or on the side. Side ladders permit faster descent if diving is not possible.

Diving boards and stands

Springboards vary in length. Short boards can be set on springs to increase flexibility. However, with increased flexibility comes decreased control. Longer boards have fixed or adjustable fulcrums.

Diving stands are available in heights of 3 meters, 1 meter, or 1/2 meter. These structures are generally assembled on sight. Both 3 meter boards and stands should be equipped with side rails. State codes determine specifications for side rails. Ladders leading to the board or platform should have hand rails as well. All diving boards and platforms should be located above water that is a safe depth for diving. Referral should be made to the National Swimming Pool Foundation Design Compendium.

Slides

Slides are exclusively used for recreational purposes. The variety of available slides and the complexity of their use is much too extensive to be covered in this book. Some state codes regulate their size and their use, and others do not. With the increase in litigation, great concerns have arisen over this piece of deck equipment. In all incidences they should be installed far enough away from diving areas and walls to ensure the safety of the participant.

For information pertaining to slides, refer to references in the bibliography.

Ladders and grabrails

Pools designed with recessed steps should be equipped with grabrails. This is the preferred design for competitive pools because it leaves lanes free of obstruction. If recessed steps are not included, ladders are needed for ease in entering an exiting the pool. Both ladders and grabrails are constructed of stainless steel tubing. If ladders and recessed steps are used for entry and exit, consideration should be given to accommodations for physically challenged patrons. Likewise, if pools are easy to get into and out of , some patrons are more apt to use it. Methods of entry then become a marketing issue.

Safety and rescue equipment

The following is a list of rescue equipment commonly found in the swimming pool area. Consideration should be given to minimum state codes.

A *ring buoy* should be located at each lifeguard station with extras on walls surrounding the pool. Buoys should be made of durable fabric with lines attached in metal anchors molded inside the ring.

Shepherd's crooks are recommended for making rescues that are close to the sides of the pool. They are manufactured in eight, twelve and sixteen foot lengths. The crook at the end of the pole should be large enough to encircle the body of an adult. These pieces of safety equipment should be hung in accessible locations. State codes determine number, placement, etc.

The National Swimming Pool Foundation Design Compendium and state codes must be consulted when designing diving boards.
(Photo: Zion Benton Twp. H.S.,courtesy of Kessler & Assoc.)

A *spineboard* made of marine plywood can be submerged so an injured person can be placed on it while still in the water. These boards should have multiple handles, sturdy nylon straps, and should be constructed so that they are raised slightly off the ground so the rescuer's hands can be placed beneath them for ease in lifting.

Safety equipment in determined by state and regional codes. These might include: first aid supplies: a resuscitator; an airway for administering artificial respiration; a portable oxygen unit; a gas mask where gas chlorine is used for chemical treatment of pool water; barrier lines dividing deep and shallow water; and signs designating restrictions and warnings. Codes should be strictly adhered to in this area.

When writing a safety plan for a pool facility, the local fire department should be involved as well. Specific procedures might be determined by the location of the facility in regard to the fire department and ambulance service. Phone numbers of emergency units should be posted alongside safety regulations and procedures.

Innovations in design

Movable or hydraulic pool floors have added much flexibility to aquatic programming especially in instances where space is limited. They are very expensive, however, and may cost more than construction of another pool. Hydraulic lift rams lower and raise a concrete bottom from as deep as ten feet to 0 feet, or flush with the pool deck in several minutes. This feature allows for adjustment of the water to the skill level of the participant. Movable floors are a great asset in working with persons with special needs.

Movable bulkheads add still more flexibility in programming and consequently increase the potential for income diversity. They allow for changing pool lengths, divisions of pool depths and separation or events.

This chapter is by no means meant to be conclusive. Design and operation of swimming pools warrants a text of its own. However, since pools are often the focal point of a recreation or fitness/wellness facility, a book about construction and operation of these would be incomplete without some mention of this area. The reader is encouraged to use the information in this chapter as an introduction to pool design, and to refer to the bibliography and state and regional codes for more specific information.

Selected Bibliography

Bronzan, R. (1974). *New concepts in planning and funding athletic physical education and recreation facilities*. Phoenix:Phonix Intermedia.

Elliott, R. (1983). Pool industry trends. *Swimming Technique, 20*, 39-42.

Gabrielsen, M. (Ed.) (1975). *Swimming pools: A guide to their planning, design and operation*. Fort Lauderdale: Hoffman.

Hunsaker, D. (1982, June). Swimming pool priorities. *Club management*, pp.15-16.

Hunsaker, D. (1983-a). Designing a natatorium. *Journal of Physical Education, Recreation & Dance, 54*, 20-21.

Hunsaker, D. (1983-b). Flexibility: A key in planning good swimming pools. *Athletic Purchasing and Facility Management, 7* 32-34, 47.

Hunsaker, D. (1983, June). Improper dives from starting blocks cause njuries. *Swimming Pool Age & Spa Merchandiser*, pp.32-33.

Hunsaker, D. (1985, March). *Parameters of design for large aquatic facilities*. Paper presented at the National Spa and Pool Institute Symposium, Indianapolis, IN.

Jaskulak, N. (1983, March). European swimming pool designs cross the Atlantic. *Parks & Recreation, 17*, 42-47.

National Swimming Pool Foundation. (1986). Design compendium for competitive swimming and diving pools (3rd ed.) San Antonio: Author.

Neuburger, D. (1984, April). Promoting and marketing public aquatic facilities. *Parks & Recreation, 10* 43-47.

Ross, B. (1984, April). Pool complex creates splash in Bernard Townsip. *Parks & Recreation, 10*, 38-42.

Shropshire, D. (1984, August). The leisure pool concept: Innovation, not renovation. *Athletic Business, 18*, 20-22.

Thompson, C. (1985, April). Public water play parks; The 'ole swimming hole revisited. *Parks & Recreation, 20*, 42-46.

Thompson, C. (1986, April). Safety managemen for water play facilities. *Parks & Recreation, 21*, 36-4-0, 74.

Manufacturers and Distributors

FW Movable Swimming Pool Floors
14760 Suite 311
Exchange National Bank Building
Olean, NY

Overly
P.O. Box 70
Greensburg, PA 15601

Paddock
P.O. Box 11676
Rock Hill, SC 29731

Recreonics
1635 Expo Lane
Indianapolis, IN 46224-5297

Stranco
P.O. Box 389
Bradley, IL 60195

10 Outdoor Equipment and Resource Centre

Equipment Centre

Every person has an inherent right to experience the excitement of the environment. Camping and the pursuit of other outdoor activities, such as canoeing, skiing, and backpacking can contribute significantly to this experience and thus to an individual's total well being. Therefore, outdoor recreation must be considered an integral part of the total wellness program and should be considered in planning certain types of facilities. Whereas health clubs or other similar facilities may not determine a need for inclusion of an area which would allow programming of such activities, educational institutions and perhaps businesses should certainly consider this provision when planning their facility.

An area which houses an inventory of outdoor equipment, such as tents, sleeping bags and other camping equipment; skis; canoes; fishing equipment; skates; etc. will provide the participant with an opportunity to borrow or rent, the necessary equipment needed to pursue outdoor activities. A Resource Centre will further provide literature and video materials which provide information regarding outdoor

adventure and trips. The inclusion of these areas will add a new dimension to a recreation or fitness/wellness facility.

Location

The outdoor equipment area should be located in a part of the facility so that it has its own entrance and thus may function as a separate unit. This will allow patrons to enter and exit without having to pass through the main building entrance or through a control access. This will also prevent transportation of camping and other outdoor equipment through lobbies, lounges and hallways.

The area should also be located adjacent to a loading dock so that deliveries can be made directly to the centre. An entrance with a wide door should open onto the dock. An overhead garage type door will allow more space, however, in cold climates this type door is extremely difficult to insulate.

Service area

The service counter should be large enough to serve two patrons simultaneously. An area at least ten feet by two feet will provide ample space for distribution of large pieces of equipment such as tents, skis, etc. For ease in maintenance, this counter should be covered with a durable melamine surface.

The service counter should be equipped with a security window that locks into the counter. This type window will provide the best security.

In addition to a service counter , an area should be designed for placement of a telephone, a cash register, and a computer terminal. Cash registers must be easily accessible for employees but far enough away from the service counter to prevent security problems. When electrical outlets are installed in this area, careful consideration must be given to the special needs of cash registers and computers.

Built-in storage space for special printed materials is an added feature in the design of the service counter. Individual bins will help with organization and distribution.

Pots, pans and lanterns can be suspended from ceiling hooks. Skis are best stored in bins while ski poles can be hung from a slotted plywood platform. They should be stored hanging from the basket. See figure 10-1.

Sleeping bags are best stored open and flat on a shelf. This will help maintain the quality of the fill. They should never be stored rolled or in stuff sacks.

Cabinets divided into cubicles provide

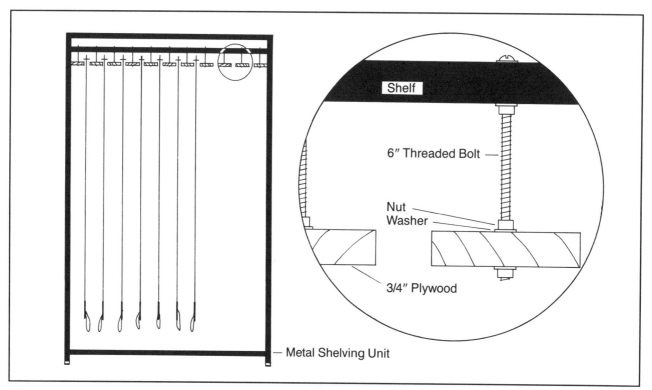

Figure 10-1: Ski Pole Storage-suggested design and construction.

Equipment storage

Utilizing maximum space is essential, therefore the use of cubic inches becomes important. Certain equipment can be hung from walls and ceiling while other types can be stored in bins, in cabinets or on shelves. Metal utility shelving units offer much versatility in this area.

the best storage for ice skates and roller skates. These cubicles must be large enough to hold skates in an upright position.

Provisions must be made for storage may be purchased and should be approved by the local fire department.

If canoes and/or other water craft are a part of the outing centre inventory, they can be stored outside the outing centre on racks which have been anchored to a concrete base. Each space should be equipped with a chain and lock so that each craft may be secured individually.

Floors

Vinyl tile, an easily maintained surface, provides a good floor for an area where spills and soiling are common. Concrete floors are less expensive and will suffice in this area. If concrete is used, it should be sealed for ease in maintenance.

Walls and ceilings

Concrete masonry units (CMUs) provide the most durable walls. They should be painted with a glossy finish so they can be easily wiped down. CMUs are less likely to chip than gypsum board or plaster walls.

Ceilings can be utilized more efficiently for storage if they are constructed of solid as opposed to acoustical tile. They should be a minimum of 12 feet high.

Lighting

Fluorescent lights recessed in the ceiling provide good lighting and are less expensive to operate than incandescent bulbs. Use of natural lighting in an area such as this can be a conservation measure.

Ventilation and exhaust

An area that houses tents, sleeping bags and other equipment used for camping purposes may have an unpleasant odor, in which case having windows that open and close will be appreciated by those working in the area. Since noxious chemicals are often used in maintenance of equipment, a good ventilation and exhaust system is essential.

Laundry facilities

Whereas laundry facilities are generally located in a separate area, they function best when placed in a room adjacent to the outing centre. The laundry room should include a washing machine, a dryer, a deep utility sink with a back splash panel, shelving above the sink for storage os supplies, shelving for towel storage and a table for folding. For removing items from washing machine to dryer, doors on each should open in a manner that will not block the passage from one to the other.

Workbench

If repairs and maintenance of equipment are to be performed within the outing centre, a workbench is essential. This surface should be 36 inches from the floor, 30 inches wide and made of sturdy material. Electrical outlets should be located above it. Pegboard mounted on the wall above the workbench and adjustable shelves will create maximum storage space. A vice secured to the bench and a built-in measuring device will prove to be useful items.

Maintenance and service equipment

Equipment that might be used in the outing centre includes a commercial sewing machine, a skate sharpener, a food dehydrator, various power tools and a ski waxer. When planning the area, consideration should be given to storage of these items.

Security system

An area which houses an extensive inventory of equipment such as an outing centre should be guarded by an individual alarm system, which operates independently of other alarm systems located within the building. A motion-sensitive system serves as a good device for determining entry to this special area. Because of this high security, it is recommended that alarm keys be assigned only to those persons who need entry clearance.

Set-up area

Whenever possible, a large room should be designated for setting up tents. This will allow for instructions on "how to" and also provide an area for checking tents when they are returned.

Outdoor Recreation Resource Centre

An outdoor recreation resource centre will be of great interest to those pursuing adventure activities. The availability of printed materials such as directories to campgrounds maps, guide books to trails and rivers, brochures containing information on state and national parks, etc. will assist adventure enthusiasts in planning outdoor pursuits. The availability of publications promoting canoeing, backpacking, skiing and other activities will stimulate interest.

Resource centres may be as simple as an information table and a materials distribution rack, or they may include video equipment for viewing informational tapes. Regardless of the degree of sophistication, the availability will be appreciated by the participant.

Even though an outdoor equipment and resource centre may not be a *top* priority area when planning a recreation or fitness/wellness facility, it will add a new dimension to any program. It not only provides an opportunity for the participant to experience the excitement of the environment but is also offers another means of generating revenue for the facility. Nominal rental rates will add to the income generated through memberships sales, court rentals, etc. Including an area such as this in the design of a new facility, or adding it to an existing one will broaden a program and contribute to the concept of total wellness.

Selected Bibliography

Austin, D. & Romisher, J. (1978, April). Towel laundering: in house or contract? *Athletic Purchasing and Facilties* 4, p.49.

Jensen, C. (1973) *Outdoor recreation in America.* Minneapolis; Burgess Publishing Company.

Parn, D. (1974) The hows and wheres of locating outdoor recreation resource information. In Manning, W. & Vos Strache, C. (Eds.) *Recreational sports programming,* pp.97-101.

Rogers, J. (1979). The development of an outdoor equipment rental for your outdoor program. In Manning, W. & Vos Strache, C. (Eds.) *Recreational sports programming,* pp.85-93.

Wash costs down the drain with on premise laundry. (1986, September). *Athletic Business,* 9 pp.48-54.

Manufacturers and Distributors

Pellerin Milnor Corporation
P.O. Box 400
Kenner, LA 70063-0400

Speed Queen
Ripton, WI 54971-0990

All Steel Inc.
(Shelving units)
14 N. First Avenue, Suite 1401
St. Charles, IL 60174

11

Locker rooms,
Public rest rooms,
and Saunas

Locker Rooms

Gone are the days when locker rooms were a dull, drab, humid cloister of steel. Today in designing locker rooms, consideration is given to aesthetic, as well as functional aspects. Locker rooms should be attractive so that participants may relax, groom themselves, and prepare to return to the world outside. Piped in music, bright music, and soft lighting help create a pleasant environment.

Locker rooms should be located centrally so they are easily accessible from all activity areas. Service centers where equipment and towels are provided should be located between men's and women's locker rooms.

The optimum size for locker rooms is debatable. The architect will have recommendations based on the projected number of users, but it is up to the building manager to estimate. A question facing all planners pertains to the size of men's facilities as compared to women's. Even though more women use recreation than ever before, this author feels that the men's locker room should be slightly larger than the women's.

Lockers

Lockers occupy a large percentage of space provided for locker rooms. It is important, therefore, to consider their placement. Placing them on concrete bases will give more space but will not allow for rearrangement of the room. Removable metal bases are less expensive than concrete and will allow for rearrangement. Lockers placed on pedestals with bench seating in front and heaters below the bench will allow warm air to help evaporate water around lockers and also warm the bench.

Variations in types of materials used in the construction of lockers is nearly as extensive as innovations in the manufacture of floor products. They can be made of steel , wood, glass, melamine, or hard plastic. However, galvanized steel lockers are still the most popular choice. A variety of colors is offered as a standard feature in all types.

The number and size of lockers is determined by the situation. If the facility is located on a university campus near residence halls, students are not as likely to use permanent locker storage. A similar facility located in an urban community will undoubtedly need more permanent locker space. The University of California at Davis used a six-to-one ratio for locker instillation, e.g. six permanent storage lockers to one transient dressing locker.

Storage lockers should be well ventilated. this allows for proper drying of clothing and shoes and decreases the odor level. Transient lockers should be long enough to prevent wrinkling of clothing. Regardless of length, lockers should be at least 15 inches deep and 12 inches wide. The larger opening is easier to get things in and out of.

Another consideration to be made when deciding types of lockers is selection of a unit with a slanted top. This type of top will not allow for collection of debris and is also easier to keep clean.

In order to facilitate locker management, the planner might consider coin operated lockers. At the University of Iowa, coin operated lockers have been a very successful addition to the facility.

Floors, Walls, and Ceilings

The type of ceilings and floor and wall surfaces selected in the construction of locker rooms is very important. Ceilings for the entire locker room area should be constructed of acoustical moisture resistant tile. Ceramic tile is probably the most popular wall and floor surface found in shower and toilet areas. It is durable, easy to maintain, non-slippery and allows for a continuous transition from floor to wall. Although non-slippery tile is most often used, synthetic flooring is gaining popularity. A poured in place synthetic material provides a monolithic surface which aids in the prevention of algae build up. These surfaces are manufactured in a variety of colors and textures.

Light fixtures should be recessed in the ceiling and vapor proof. Controls should be key operated and located in a dry area. Emergency lighting should also be included. For information on lighting, refer to Chapter 3.

Carpeting is an ideal surface for dressing areas. It provides an attractive atmosphere, is

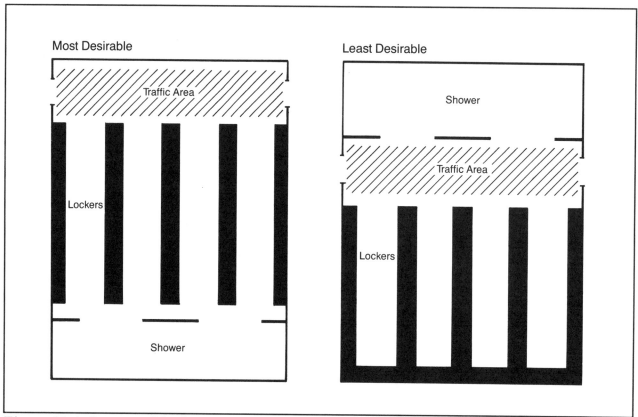

Figure 11-1: Suggested locker room layout.

warm and is likewise easy to maintain. Carpeted areas should be located far enough away from showers to prevent constant saturation. Also areas where barefoot traffic walks to and from showers should not cross heavily-used walk ways from entrances and exits (see figure 11-1).

Shower and rest room areas should be equipped with a hose bib and a floor drain for easy maintenance. Floors should also be sloped toward drains. Carpeted floors need not be sloped since hosing is not needed for cleaning purposes.

Showers

The number of showers and type is determined by the situation. This number can be based on the assumption that showers usually take ten to fifteen minutes. This assumption along with estimation of peak load will help in determining the number of shower heads needed.

The open shower is the most popular and economical type of shower in institutional locker rooms. Shower heads may be located on walls, but even more economical are those located on poles. If this type is selected, four heads are recommended. A private shower stall should be provided for individuals who do not wish to bathe in public. To ensure privacy, curtains may also be included. This addition will increase maintenance. Eventually curtains will collect soap scum and water deposits.

Shower heads should be adjustable. Nothing is more annoying than taking a shower underneath a hard penetrating flow of water, or an extremely fine mist that scarcely allows the user to rinse soap from the body.

Recessed liquid soap dispensers located through the shower area offer a safe method for dispensing soap. Some individuals will prefer using their own soap, so in addition soap dishes should be provided.

Temperature and humidity

Humidity control and temperature are important considerations for the comfort of the user and for maintenance of th area. Humidity must be controlled in order to prevent condensation which will cause maintenance problems. Humidity should be less than 60 percent and temperature should be approximately 80 degrees Fahrenheit.

Some steam will escape from shower areas even with the best ventilating systems, therefore grooming areas should be located far enough from showers so that steam does not accumulate on mirrors. A battery-operated fresh air dispenser located in grooming areas will help eliminate odors.

Mirrors

Mirrors should be placed above lavatories and in other locations as well. When they are placed above lavatories only, congestions may occur. A good location for full length mirrors is the end of locker banks.

Hair dryers

Hair dryers should be included in both men's and women's locker rooms. These should be located at varying heights and should have rotating nozzles as opposed to fixed nozzles. Nozzles which swivel 360 degrees add convenience to hair drying.

In addition to wall mounted hair dryers, outlets should be provided near mirrors for those patrons who choose to use hand held hair dryers. These will also be used for electric razors.

Toilet Area

The same considerations should be given toilet areas located in locker rooms as those for public rest rooms. If possible, toilets and urinals should be located in an enclosure separate from lavatories.

Saunas

Once reserved for athletes, today saunas are being include in the construction of most recreation and fitness/wellness facilities. They aid in relaxation, tension reduction, and contribute to the total well being of the individual. Saunas are easy to construct and relatively inexpensive. They occupy a small area and require no special plumbing.

Saunas can be made of redwood, hemlock, cedar, aspen or pine. Redwood and cedar are most often used for walls, ceilings, and benches. floors should be concrete. A removable wood slotted rack covering the concrete floor is recommended.

Saunas are potentially dangerous, therefore every precaution should be taken to ensure safety. Temperature controls should be located outside the sauna and be inaccessible to the bather. Timer switches with a maximum of 30 minutes should also be located on the outside wall. The heater, located inside the sauna, should be enclosed in a wood fence. The door should open out and have a window for viewing inside. Warnings concerning safe use should be posted on the sauna door. These should include potential danger to older persons and persons with poor health.

Public rest rooms

Public rest rooms should be located near the main entrance of the building and close to administrative offices. They should be attractive easy to maintain and provide conveniences for the public.

Floors and walls

Ceramic tile provides an attractive, easily maintained surface for floors and walls in public rest rooms (See Chapter 1). A floor drain should be installed for cleaning purposes.

Partitions

Partitions separating and/or urinals may be made of stainless steel, porcelain enamel, marble or plastic laminate. All are easy to clean. Marble, stainless steel and plastic laminate are not as easily defaced as an enamel surface. Plastic laminate is least expensive.

Installation of partitions may be more important than the choice of material selected. Ceiling hung partitions provide a floor free from obstacles to speed maintenance design and construction may dictate the type of installation.

Fixtures

Toilets, urinals and sinks should be made of durable materials. Stainless steel plumbing fixtures are suitable for rest rooms where vandalism may be a problem. Fixtures mounted to walls will help in floor maintenance. It is easier to keep floors around toilets and sinks clean if there are no floor supports.

Accessories

Electric hand dryers are more economical, litter free, and sanitary than paper towels. They

Either model will be appreciated by the janitorial staff. Keep in mind that electrical appliances need servicing periodically.

Paper towels are probably the choice of the user for hand drying but may be a cause of major irritation to the maintenance staff, the user and consequently to the building manager. The type of dispenser chosen can save money and prevent irritability.

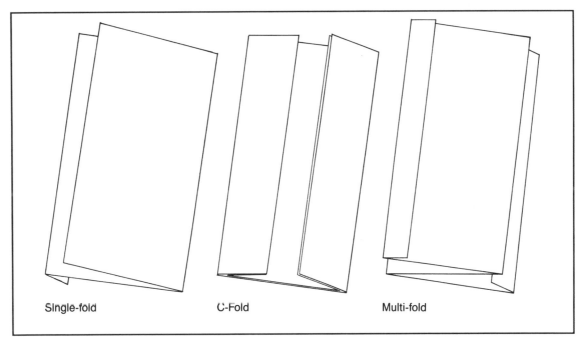

Single-fold   C-Fold   Multi-fold

Figure 11-2: Single-fold, c-fold, and multi- fold paper towels.

may be mounted on the wall or recessed into the wall to help in preventing vandalism. Push button models with swivel nozzles for use in face drying are most frequently selected, however, "no touch" models are becoming more popular. They provide maximum efficiency and sanitation. An infrared sensor activates the unit when the user's hands are placed below the exhaust port. The dryer then stops automatically when user's hands are removed.

There are several types of dispensers that distribute folded towels, e.g. multi-fold, c-fold, and single fold. (see figure 11-2). Multi-fold and single fold will dispense one towel at a time. C-fold have a tendency to dispense several, and consequently create litter and waste. Roll type dispensers allow the user to dispense as much towel as needed.

Waste receptacles should be conveniently located for the user, large enough to hold the amount of waste they will receive between maintenance shifts, and convenient for the janitorial staff. Combination towel dispenser/ trash receptacles are often too small to accommodate the volume of trash they will receive. Consequently users will deposit trash elsewhere. Free standing waste receptacles are easier to empty than models that are built into the wall or beneath counter tops. Push top torpedo cans are recommended and preferred by most custodial staffs.

Napkin disposal units may be surface mounted to a partition inside each toilet enclosure or recessed inside a partition to serve two compartments. These units are equipped with push- flap doors. The single unit system increases maintenance time but may be more durable in the long run. Surface mounted units often provide an additional shelf, a feature appreciated by some users.

Soap dispenser units may distribute liquid, lather, or powdered soap. They should be carefully located in order to be functional. Those located on sinks or counter tops may not allow enough space for the user to place hands underneath for dispensing, therefore wallmounted units will probably be more serviceable.

From a maintenance standpoint, dispensers that are easily filled are the choice of the janitorial staff. Likewise drip-free units are also appreciated by those who clean. Units dispensing lather and powder drip less than those dispensing liquid soap.

Toilet tissue holders, like paper towel dispensers can have a great effect on maintenance and commodities costs. Strangely

enough, toilet tissue seems to be a prime item for theft in public rest rooms, therefore theft-resistant units are preferable.

Two types of toilet tissue are available-roll and sheet. Rolled paper is much more economical and by far preferred by the user. Sheets are poor in quality and very difficult to remove from the dispenser. Consequently, the user will remove several sheets simultaneously creating waste and a litter problem.

Rolled dispensers may be surface mounted, recessed, single, double, side-by-side, or piggy-back. Piggy-back rolls (one housed on top of the other) have a tendency to jam, causing problems with dispensing. Single rolls will need to be replaced more often. Recessed double roll, side-by-side models will probably provide the most efficient distribution of tissue.

Mirrors and shelves should be placed above each sink. Mirrors are, of course, an accessory we can't do without, and shelves are another convenience.

All fixtures and accessories in public rest rooms should be accessible to handicapped persons. Even though architects are very much aware of these regulations, occasionally oversights are made. The user must live with these errors after construction is complete. An oversight which often occurs is the height of mirrors for wheelchair users.

Whereas the public rest room facilities may seem of lesser importance to the manager of the facility than other areas, they can become a source of major irritation and a time-consuming concern from a management standpoint if they are not properly designed and maintained. The latter depends much on the former, therefore careful consideration should be given in the selection of flooring and walls, fixtures and accessories.

Selected Bibliography

A conceptual approach to facility planning. (1986, July) *Athletic Business*, p.74.

Colberg,G. (1981) Locker installation at University of California/Davis campus. *NIRSA Journal, 6.*

Could a sauna room contribute to your conditioning program? (1978, April). *Athletic Purchasing and Facilities.*, p.52.

Looking good locker rooms. (1986, April). *Athletic Business*, p.4.

Penman, K. (1977). *Planning physical education & athletic facilities in schools.* New York: John Wiley & Sons.

Penman, K. (1983, April). Upgrading your locker, shower,and laundry facilities. *Athletic Purchasing and Facilities.* p.16.

The new locker room: pampering the clientele. (1985, April) *Athletic Business.*, p.38.

Tips on designing functional locker rooms. (1981,September). *Athletic Purchasing and Facilities*, p.4

Manufacturers and Distributors

Accurate Partitions Corp.
8000 Joliet Road
McCook, IL 60525

American Locker Security Systems
P.O. Box 489
Jamestown, NY 14702-0489

Best Lock Corporation
P.O. Box 50444
Indianapolis, IN 40250

Bradley
Washroom Accessories Division
Mt. Laurel, NJ 08054

Bradmax
Vandal Resistant Plumbing Fixtures
P.O. Box 309
Menomonee Falls, WI 53051

Cabrillant
W & W Glass Products Ltd.
Spring Valley, NY 10977

Electric-Aire Corporation
27740 Avenue Hopkins
Valencia, CA 91355

Fiberesin
Personal Storage Units
Fibresin Industries, Inc.
Oconomowoc, WI 53066

Holloman
Wood Lockers by Holloman
Edmond, OK 73034

Mini Check
American Locker Security Systems
Jamestown, NY 14701

Republic Storage Systems
1038 Belden Ave. N.E.
Canton, OH 44705

Universal Distributions
Health and Fitness Products
930 27th Avenue, S. W.
Cedar Rapids, IA 52406.

12

Service Areas

The service areas described in this chapter are sometimes referred to as the central core of the facility. They include the entry way, the administrative offices and conference room, the service window and the lounge area. These areas are often the first seen by patrons and may set the tone for acceptance or rejection of the facility. It is therefore equally as important to properly design and furnish these areas as it is to do likewise with activity areas. The purpose of this chapter is to provide information which will assist in creating an environment conducive to administrative duties, serving the public, and lounging.

Entry ways and service windows

The entry way is the most utilized area in the entire facility. No matter which play area participants plan to use, they must all enter through a common entrance. It may set the mood for all those entering whether participant or employee. For this reason care must be taken to ensure an efficient, easily maintained attractive space.

Double foyers are extremely important in areas of the country where temperatures are cold. They also allow an extra area for cleaning shoes. Permanently recessed floor treads and floor mats allow dirt, mud and slush to fall into the area beneath them. The grid is permanently installed whereas the mat may be rolled back to facilitate cleaning. These recessed surfaces significantly reduce floor maintenance in hallways. Treads may be carpeted, aluminum, vinyl, or various kinds of abrasive grids. A tread with an abrasive finish is best for an entry way.

Signage is important throughout the building, especially in the entry way. Signs that are permanently made, as opposed to those fashioned from poster board and markers, are more attractive and will last longer. These may include messages such as "no smoking," or hours of building operation. Too many signs clutter the area, and those entering consequently will not read them.

Permanent signs are often mounted to doors or windows, but they may also be placed on movable stands. Types of signs are covered in Chapter 14.

Controlling entry to the facility may or may not be the choice of the building occupants. If controlled entry is essential, the turnstile will contribute to the ease of managing this task, allowing only one person to enter at a time. It also can serve as a means of counting the number of users, or eliminating the need for a door attendant. The sophisticated system at Southern Illinois University-Carbondale controls entry without the assistance of a door attendant and counts the number of entries hour by hour.

Users are issued a plastic card that serves as a key to the turnstile. This computerized system furnishes other information, such as category of user, e.g. faculty, community member, student, etc. A system such as this although initially very expensive, will eventually pay for itself in personnel service dollars.

Trash receptacles and containers used for extinguishing smoking materials should be located outside the main entrance. Bike racks likewise should be located in front of the building.

Service windows

The service window is located adjacent to the administrative office for convenience in communication between the two areas, and also indirect view of those entering the building. It should serve as a counter for the patron and service area and storage space for the attendant. Therefore the design is of utmost importance. As a counter, it must be high enough for the patron to perform tasks such as writing, and as a storage space it must contain cubicles beneath for easy access to materials that will be distributed to the patron. It should also be designed so that the worker does not have a long reach to serve the patron.

The material used in the construction of the counter is important because of the constant wear. Patrons have a tendency to lean against walls beneath counters causing scratches and nicks. Belt buckles and book bags are the biggest culprits. Durable wall covering and tile are much better choices than plaster. The top should be constructed of melamine or an equally durable, easily maintained surface.

Sliding glass windows equipped with security locks are probably the best means of enclosing the service area. This allows visibility and light to enter the area even if windows are closed.

Administrative offices and Conference rooms

A pleasant work environment is essential to productivity. Proper lighting, comfortable temperatures and air circulation, desirable colors, and certain conveniences all have an important role in creating a work place conducive to productive activity. Work effectiveness studies to date have primarily concentrated on industrial environments rather than office environments. It is much easier to account for productivity when measurable items are involved, e.g. number of products coming off assembly lines. Recent research pertaining to office workers has taken a look at attendance, efficiency, and interpersonal relationships with fellow workers. Findings indicate that satisfaction with the work environment plays an important role in job performance. In this chapter, the following aspects of the work environment will be examined: lighting, aesthetics, temperature and ventilation, furnishings, and conveniences.

Lighting

Lighting is one of the most important aspects of the office environment. Studies have shown that workers' evaluation of office lighting, and office conditions in general were influenced by the level of illumination. Also natural lighting was found to be an important factor contributing to environmental satisfaction. Windows not only provide additional light, but they also reduce perceived crowding, offer contact with the outside world, and provide a focal point for visual relief.

The overhead fluorescent fixture provides a good source of artificial light for offices and conference rooms. As previously mentioned, it is economical, long lasting and suitable for desk work. Incandescent lamps, either floor models or table models, give the employee lighting they can adjust and also suggest a warm, residential look.

Natural lighting contributes to energy efficiency and is preferred because psychologically, people like to have an external point of reference to tell the weather or time of day. Skylights and windows are both good sources of natural light. Windows should have attractive covering so light can be controlled. Both vertical and horizontal blinds are very popular and provide a more easily maintained covering than curtains or drapes.

Aesthetics

Colors can and do create moods. Generally speaking, greens seem to be cooling and act as a sedative, whereas yellows are stimulating. On dark and gloomy days, when the yellow of the sun is missing, people have a tendency to be sluggish and when the sun reappears, they become more active both mentally and physically. Red is exciting and stimulates the brain, purple is a sedative and orange has a stimulating effect. The occupant of an office with an orange wall may become ill at ease after a short time and feel the necessity to leave. Individuals who work in cool-colored rooms may complain about the air-conditioning, while others who work in rooms of the same temperature with warm-colored walls will complain that there is no air-conditioning.

The selection of colors and their placement in the office should be carefully considered. These include the choice of wall colors, carpet color and design, and the color of furniture fabric. The potential occupant should work closely with the architect in choosing color combinations that are suitable for the area. All colors must relate to each other and to a central scheme, so personal choice among staff may complicate decisions.

Accessories add visual stimulation to the surroundings. They should relate to the interest of the owner and fit into the design of the room. They may take the form of sculpture, photographs, paintings, prints, drawings, or plants. If two dimensional art work is selected, it should be attractively framed and hung tastefully. Enlarged photographs, professionally matted and framed are an attractive and inexpensive means of decorating wall space.

Silk plants are a medium for adding greenery to offices and conference rooms, but they are expensive. Polyester plants are becoming more popular and are less expensive. The merits of artificial plants are their lack of need for care and the versatility in placing them anywhere regardless of light source. Live plants are much more economical, but require care and proper lighting for survival.

Conveniences

Conveniences include a potpourri of accommodations designed to meet the needs of the user. Technology would have it that most of us are using machines now to help us become more efficient. Work stations other than desks may be needed for computers. Consideration may be given to built-in desks for this purpose in main administrative offices and in work rooms. This will alleviate the need for additional furniture.

There is never enough storage space. This phenomenon is one of Murphy's most accurate predictions. We must keep trying however, to prove it wrong in planning for as much storage space as possible in the original design. Wherever possible, cabinets should be built above and below for storage of office supplies. The design of these cabinets can create usable counter tops as additional work space.

It should never be assumed that architects consider placement of electrical outlets and telephone jacks a matter of convenience for the user. Inquiries should be made as to their placement and to the number in each office. The arrangement of phone and electrical outlets will dictate the arrangement of office furniture and the ability to use more than one machine. Consideration should be given to voltage as well. If the worker uses a calculator, a typewriter, and a desk lamp simultaneously will it cause a power failure from overload?

Another convenience consideration is the arrangement of the office suite. Are offices easily accessible for circulation among staff? Are rest rooms likewise accessible? Is there a room or space for storage of coats and boots.

Background music may or may not be considered a convenience depending on individual control. If the individual has control it can be as stimulating as visual effects in the office. However, if there is no choice it can be a source of irritation, so individual controls should be provided in each office. If at all possible, consideration should be given to separate sound systems for offices and the remainder of the building. It is likely that office staff will not choose to listen to the same type of music that participants choose.

The need for privacy depends on how information gathering and dissemination take place. Partitions may serve this purpose in creating visual privacy, but they will not work if complete privacy is needed.

Furniture

The desk is the most important piece of furniture in the office. Therefore, it should be comfortable and provide the maximum amount of work surface. The rectangular shaped desk is the least efficient but the most popular. The modified L-shape is more efficient, therefore it is often used by secretaries.

Many executives are choosing a table type finding that is is more conducive for informal meetings than the traditional desk. If the executive chooses a conventional type desk, an overhang on the visitor's side should be considered. This puts the visitor closer to the desk.

There are two types of file cabinets: vertical files in which the drawer is filled from front to back; and lateral files in which the drawer is filled from side to side. The lateral file protrudes less into the work area and has a more contemporary look. It may also provide additional work space.

Seating discomfort can affect productivity and health, therefore chairs should be carefully selected. Executives may spend minimal time at their desks and therefore choose highback impressive chairs, whereas secretaries and other workers will spend hours sitting in the same position and need a much more ergonomically sound chair. Armrests can aid in shifting weight and offer some support to the back, however they may restrict movement. Executives will likely choose a chair with armrests whereas a secretary may not. The shape and size of conference room furniture is often chosen to fit the space it will occupy. The rectangular table is the most popular and hierarchical. Shaping the table slightly wider at its middle allows everyone to see and hear. The round table encourages participation but requires a larger space. Chairs with armrests should fit comfortably around the table. The number of persons using the conference room at any given time should be considered before selecting table size and number of chairs.

Respect and concern for a happy, productive staff will be reflected in the planning and design of offices and conference rooms. It is equally as important as the "play space" created for the participant.

Lounges

A question often asked is "should space be devoted to a lounge?" And if so, what should be included in it? A television? Game tables?

What is include will depend on the situation. If televisions and ping-pong tables are available to participants in other buildings or in other parts of the recreation facility, they need not be included. Televisions especially tend to attract crowds at certain times of the day. It is this author's opinion that they are best suited for other facilities.

The lounge area is an area designed for relaxation after activity, an area for visitors to sit while waiting for appointments or a place for social gatherings, both spontaneous and planned. It's the "living room" of the recreation facility. Therefore it should be designed and furnished as such.

Furniture

In choosing furniture for the lounge, durable fabrics that require minimal care should be selected. Good synthetic fibers are acceptable, however, heavy weight cotton blends or wool wear longer and are easier to repair. Tufting (buttons) should be avoided. Quality is the key to selection.

Protective finishes are available which will encourage soil resistance. These are more effective if factory applied. Upholstery should be flame resistant.

Solid, dark fabrics tend to reveal lint, while solid white fabrics show soil. Therefore, the use of woven fabrics is a better choice. It may be necessary to use some solid colors to accentuate or promote a dominant color theme. Furniture trimmed in wood should be avoided. Wood trim often encourages vandalism.

The addition of casters on furniture legs allows pieces to be moved about easily. This may or may not be a desirable characteristic. The size of individual pieces of furniture will encourage or discourage extended lounging (sleeping). Couch size pieces provide a large enough area for loungers to completely recline whereas groupings of chair size pieces will encourage intended use of the area.

Lighting

Both natural and artificial lighting can enhance the aesthetic quality of a lounge area. Natural lighting form windows or skylights should supply as much of the illumination as possible. In cold climates, large glass areas should be oriented to the south or southeast. This should contribute to a warm temperature. Skylights will provide the same light and warmth and are therefore energy efficient, however, if not properly constructed and installed, they have a tendency to leak.

The addition of artificial light will add to the balance of illumination. The ceiling mounted fluorescent bulb is probably the least expensive to operate and will supply adequate lighting for all areas. Table lamps will add to the warmth and aesthetic beauty of the room.

Flooring

In order to ensure continuity, the floor surface for the lounge area should be the same as that used for the main entry way and traffic areas. An addition of area rugs might be a consideration, however this will increase maintenance time and costs.

Walls

Wall treatment in the lounge area is probably more important than wall construction. If walls are made of gypsum board (as most are), they may be decorated

Tables and chairs in the vending area will encourage patrons to confine eating to this area.*(photo:Simon Center, St. Louis University, courtesy of Hastings & Chivetta Architects, Inc.)*

with wallcovering. A plain paper, as opposed to a patterned one, allows more flexibility in design. However, a mural decoration can be an interesting substitute for a movable piece of art work. Movable artwork can create an ambience that murals cannot. Suggestions for artwork include paintings and prints, banners and wall hangings, and photography.

Clock

A clock should be mounted on a wall high enough so that it can be viewed from all seating arrangements. The face and numerals should be large enough so they can be read from a distance. More information is available on clocks in Chapter 14.

Plants

In an area where natural lighting has been utilized, live plants provide an inexpensive addition to the lounge. Depending on the size of the area, large plants can be used. A few large plants take less time to maintain than many smaller ones.

Vending area

The vending areas should be located near the lounge and the main entrance of the building. This allows patrons to purchase food or beverage and consume it in a controlled area or take it with them as they exit the building.

Machines

Decisions about the contents of the machines should be made by the building manager. Machines should include healthful foods as well as "junk food." Contents might include yogurt, fruit, juices as well as pop and candy. Gum is not a good choice for obvious reasons. Beverages dispensed in cups cause fewer maintenance problems than those dispensed in cans. The addition of ice is usually preferred by the thirsty patron. Machines which dispense hot beverages such as coffee, tea, or soup are not as popular as cold beverage machines. A change machine located near vending machines will eliminate many trips made to the service window. If vending areas are located near a supervisor's station, vandalism of change machines and vending machines should not be a problem.

Furniture

An arrangement of tables and chairs in the vending room will encourage patrons to eat their purchases in the vending area. This of course, requires extra space which may not be available. A room sixteen feet by sixteen feet will accommodate four vending machines, two tables 40 inches in diameter and eight chairs.

Flooring

When choosing the floor surface for the vending area, select a material that can withstand spills. Usually the same flooring is used in this area as that used in hallways and high traffic areas. Tile is a better surface than carpeting.

Trash receptacles

Trash receptacles should be placed in the area. They should be large enough to accommodate waste accumulation between custodial shifts. A torpedo can with a swinging lid is a good choice.

Service areas which provide a comfortable environment for staff and patrons contribute much to the successful operation of recreation and fitness/wellness facilities.

Suggested Bibliography

Ball, V. (1982). *The art of interior design.* New York: John Wiley & Sons.
Halse, A. (1968) *The use of color in interiors.* New York: McGraw Hill Book Company.
Yee, R. & Gustafson, K. (1983). *Corporate design.* New York: Van Nostrand Reinhold Company.

Manufacturers and Distributors

Alvarado Manufacturing Company
Turnstiles
9630 Fern Street, S.
El Monte, CA 91732

Turfmat
Construction Specialties, Inc.
P.O.Box 380
Muncy, PA, 17756

Publix Office Supplies
700 W Chicago Ave.
Chicago, IL 60610

E & I Office Supplies
180 Froehlich Farm Road
Woodbury, NY 11797

Mosler Safe Company
5693 Howard St.
Niles, IL 60648

13

Miscellaneous Features

Public telephones

At least one public, coin operated telephone should be located in a facility. Additional phones may be needed depending on the size of the facility. In either case, at least one must be accessible to handicapped persons. The location of public phones is determined at the blueprint phase in a new construction project or by the "walk-through" method when renovating existing facilities. Local telephone companies can provide information regarding installation and service of coin operated phones.

Fire extinguishers

All fire equipment should be approved by local fire departments and checked regularly for quality assurance. A multi-purpose dry chemical extinguisher will extinguish all classifications of fires (A: wood, paper and cloth; B: liquids and gases; C: electrical). These should be large enough so they may not be confiscated in gym bags and should be housed in cabinets that are clearly marked.

Security system

Selection of security systems can become quite complicated. Before choosing, those responsible for managment of a facility should visit other facilities and inquire about the efficiency of systems regulating entry and egress.

> **Features of various systems include but are not limited to the following:**
> 1. **Doors that allow egress but will alarm if not deactivated.**
> 2. **Doors that will not allow egress unless fire alarms are activated.**
> 3. **Control panels that are located at a supervisory control station which indicate the area in which alarm sounds.**
> 4. **Motion sensors which may be activated to prevent movement in a certain area. (These may be best suited for equipment storage areas.)**
> 5. **Heat sensors which may be activated to prevent entry into certain areas.**

Any combination of these features may be selected. The managers of the facility should work with architects to determine the most efficient system. There are certain advantages and disadvantages to all features. For instance, if control access is monitored by a system that allows for egress at all doors, but sounds an alarm if not deactivated, persons may enter or exit without being apprehended. Likewise, motion alarms are often very sensitive and may give warning if balls roll from shelves or if plants move from air circulation in the area. Heat sensors work better in areas such as these.

All security alarm systems should be monitored by local law enforcement authorities during hours when the facility is not open. Otherwise, alarm systems controlling entry and egress can be monitored by a supervisor stationed near an indicator panel.

Communication centers

Communication centers include all the visual tools needed for presentations stored in an enclosed cabinet. Various combinations of features might be selected to include cork tack board, markerboard, chalkboard, flip charts and projection screens. These units vary in size from approximately 6 feet by 4 feet, to 2 feet by 4 feet. Communication centers are ideal for conference rooms and rooms where groups assemble for presentations.

Bulletin boards

Glass enclosed bulletin boards are preferred for display in areas available to the public. Heavy gauge aluminum frames enclosed with tempered glass doors equipped with flat key tumbler locks provide a safe and attractive means of displaying announcements, schedules, etc. Backings are made of a variety of materials including fabric or cork. Units may also be recessed inside walls or surface mounted. Manufacturer's specifications should be carefully adhered to when ordering these untis.

Display cases

Display cases are most often included in recreation and fitness/wellness facilities for exhibiting trophies, awards; and craft projects, in facilities where creative art centres are located. Types of cases include freestanding, recessed wall, surface mounted wall, and table. Most

have sliding glass doors with locks and some are luminated. Cases built into the wall occupy less space and provide less maintenance concerns. Many optional features can alter the function and appearance of a display case. Therefore, when ordering from a vendor, specify not only size but the type of frame, width of shelving and depth of case.

Clocks

An important feature to remember when installing clocks in a facility, is the size of the clock in relationship to the size of the area. For instance, a twelve inch clock is of little use to a swimmer in an enormous pool area if it is mounted high above the deck. Careful placement of smaller clocks in large areas may compensate for this problem.

The clock lens should be unbreakable. Dials should also be shatterproof. Injection molded cases with no seams provide a more substantial housing. Other features to consider include a second hand, a computerized timing device, and a luminated dial. If clocks are not installed as part of an institutional timing system, they should be quartz battery operated.

Bicycle racks

Bicycle racks should be carefully selected to accommodate all types of bikes. The wedge loading design can accommodate wide or narrow tier vehicles and larger handle bars and additional accessories if wedges are spaced 24 to 30 inches apart. These racks may be permanently embedded in concrete, eliminating ground bars which have a tendency to collect leaves and trash.

There are many different types of rack designs to choose from, but the same considerations should be given to all. They include: size of bikes to be accommodated; durability of construction; and installation. Careful selection and placement of these accessories will help eliminate bicycle clutter from sidewalks and other areas.

Coat hooks

Coat hooks installed on gymnasium walls (and in other areas where participants might leave outer clothing on floors,) not only help keep areas free from a cluttered appearance, but also help provide a safer environment for play. In gymnasiums, participants have a tendency to lay outerwear alongside courts creating a potentially dangerous situation. Hooks installed on walls high enough above the floor and in recessed ares, will encourage participants to store garments there. Signs should be posted above these accessories that free management of all responsibilities from theft.

Signage

Visual communication systems are usually developed, constructed, and installed by professionals. However, information must be supplied by the occupant. Signs should provide a clear message for the intended viewer. These messages include orientation and information, identification, warnings and prohibitory messages and official notices.

In a newly constructed facility, location of signs should be determined with blueprints. For renovation of exisiting facilities, the "walk-through" method is best for determining location. In the "walk-through" method the role of the visitor should be assumed.

Indoor signs

Indoor signs should include a directory, located inside the main entrance of the facility; directional signs and those identifying room numbers or names; no entry signs and official notice signs such as emergency and evacuation procedures. Changeable signs such as directories should be vandalproof and unexposed to removal by unauthorized personnel. Directories are usually constructed of anodized aluminum with grooved felt or cork backgrounds. These backgrounds may be available in a variety of colors, however black is standard and usually preferred. They may be freestanding or recessed inside a wall. Plastic letters are available in sizes ranging from approximately 3 inches to 3/8 inches. Storage boxes should be included with orders for letters.

Announcements and other information that may change on a regular basis can be inexpensively and attractively displayed under permanently mounted plexiglass sheets. These can be attached to walls or doors.

Outdoor signs

Outdoor signs should include any directional information, signs for parking, handicapped accessibility and the name of the facility. The same principle applies to location for outdoor signs. In the case of newly constructed facilities, location is determined at the blueprint phase while the "walk-thorugh" method is used in renovation.

Suggested Bibliography

McClendon, C. & Blackston, M. (1982) *Signage*. New York: McGraw-Hill Book Company.

Manufacturers and Distributors

Loader racks
Bicycle racks
604 Glover
Urbana, IL 61801

Howard Miller
Clocks
Zeeland, MI 49464

Claridge
Projection Screens
Harrison, AR 72602

Clean City Square, Inc.
Outdoor Trash Receptacles
P.O. Box 6797
St. Louis, MO 63144

Hardwood Visuals
Communication Centers
530 5th Ave.
New Brighton, MN 55112

J.L. Industries
Fire Extinguishers
4450 W. 78th Street Circle
Bloomington, MN 55435

Lathem Time Recorder Co.
168 Selig Drive, S.W.
Atlanta, GA 30378

Oasis (Water Cooler)
Ebco Manufacturing Co.
265 N. Hamilton Road
Columbus, OH 43213-0150

OPERATIONS

Section III

The final section of this book addresses the operations of the newly constructed or renovated facility. The following issues will be covered: formulating building policies; training staff; public relations and marketing; and maintenance.

14

Maintenance

The construction or renovation of recreation and or fitness/wellness facilities creates not only a new and exciting environment for the participant, but also a new environment for those responsible for care and maintenance of these facilities. Because many new and innovative surfaces are being used in the construction of these buildings, maintenance personnel often find themselves uninformed as to the proper procedure for cleaning. It is the manager's responsibility to see that the custodial staff is informed if special care is needed.

Cleaning costs consume a large portion of an operating budget. Much of this can be attributed to labor. Therefore, effective cleaning practices not only preserve equipment and facilities but also save labor cost. The design of custodial areas, the selection of equipment and supplies, staffing and training as well as cleaning methods all contribute to effective and efficient cleaning.

Custodial service areas

Custodial areas must be designed with the concept of built-in cleanability. With the rise in labor costs over the last few years, those responsible for custodial management must assert themselves during the design stage in order to ensure the inclusion of adequate janitorial space. In designing this space consideration should be given to location, floors, walls and ceilings, doors and entry ways, plumbing fixtures, and storage.

Ideally, the main custodial service area should be centrally located. Individual closets should be located throughout the facility so that no area of the building is more than 150 feet away from a mop sink. No mechanical equipment, electric panels, etc. should be located inside custodial areas.

Floors in custodial areas should be either vinyl tile or concrete. If a concrete floor is installed, it should be sealed for easy maintenance and durability.

Walls and ceilings should be constructed of impervious material. Concrete masonry units (CMUs) painted with high gloss enamel provide an excellent wall surface that is not easily chipped or stained. Ceilings likewise may be made of concrete and should be high enough (10 feet) for clearance of long broom and mop handles. Light fixtures should ideally be recessed in the ceiling, however if ceilings are high enough, this may not be necessary.

Doors and entry ways should be wide enough for transportation of large pieces of equipment into and out of the area. Double doors with removable mullions will provide as much as 72 inches of space. A doorway leading outside the building and close to a loading dock will facilitate delivery of equipment and supplies.

Plumbing fixtures located inside the custodial service area include a floor type basin with a 6 inch basin curb. Hot and cold water outlets should be located approximately 24 inches above the basin.

Adequate storage space is essential in this area. It should include an area large enough to store 55 gallon drums of cleaning liquids, shelving which will accommodate storage of supplies in case lots, and cabinets that lock. Pegs for hanging certain items and hangers should be located over the basin for storage of wet mops. Provisions should also be made for storing ladders.

The central area should contain provisions for secure storage of custodial staff's personal belongings (coat racks, locks, etc.), and a table and chairs for eating meals. A telephone in this area is an added convenience that will be appreciated. Policies governing use of the telephone should be posted in the area.

Staffing

Staffing is usually determined by the building services department in educational institutions. However, in some institutions of higher education and in private entities, staffing may be the responsibility of the building manager.

According to the *Basic manual for physical plant administration,* custodial staff can be assigned 15,000 square feet of space per janitor. This is the simplest method but it fails to identify the difference in types of spaces to be maintained. When custodians are assigned to

certain areas they seem to take more pride in their work. Work also becomes less monotonous, morale is kept high and consequently turnover is reduced. If this method is to be utilized the manager should identify the areas to be cleaned, assign individuals to the areas and time them. Averaging the times of several workers in similar areas will enable the manager to make assignments accordingly.

Training is extremely important, especially in facilities with surfaces and areas that may be foreign to custodial staff. The use of video training tapes prepared in-house will help janitors work with many of the new and innovative products used in construction of recreation and fitness/wellness facilities. In preparing training sessions, the manager should rely on manufacturers' recommendations for cleaning. These are specified in printed materials available through the manufacturer.

Equipment and supplies

Adequate equipment is essential to good cleaning practices. If the custodial staff is given inferior equipment, too little equipment, manual equipment instead of power equipment, they are less than enthusiastic about their work and will eventually cost the establishment money. High costs of labor can most often be attributed to inadequate equipment. Quantity and quality are important when selecting maintenance equipment. Quality ensures longer lasting equipment and quantity helps ensure more efficient use of time.

Methods for cleaning special surfaces

Floors

Wood floors can be maintained easily and will retain their beauty for many years if cared for properly. They should be mopped with an oil treated dust mop daily. Water should never be used on the surface for cleaning. Floors should also be checked daily for scuff marks. When marks are present, they should be removed by dry buffing with an electric buffer followed by mopping with an oil treated dust mop. Heavy marks may need to be removed with "finish remover." This should be applied with a soft cloth.

Rubber floors are tough and durable, but more difficult to clean than wood floors. Most manufacturers recommend that rubber be vacuumed once a week and scrubbed twice a year. Whereas this may be a feasible solution for large installations such as gymnasiums, other rooms, (e.g. weight/exercise rooms,) will need to be cleaned more often. These areas may need to be vacuumed every other day and scrubbed at least once a week in order to maintain them properly. Floors should be cleaned with a detergent and water applied with a floor scrubber. All excess water should be removed with a mop.

Surfaces made of PVC are cleaned in the same manner as rubber floors, although they may not need to be scrubbed as frequently as rubber floors.

Because brick tiles such as quarry tile are generally used in high traffic areas, they should be swept and mopped with a detergent daily or as needed. A floor scrubber with an extractor will speed the cleaning process. Brick tile floors should never be waxed.

Vinyl tile should be swept daily, mopped once a week and waxed twice a year or as needed. Scuff marks can be removed with an abrasive back sponge. Care should be taken, however, not to scratch the tile.

Ceramic tile is most often used in locker rooms and rest rooms and therefore should be maintained daily to prevent the growth of bacteria. All areas around toilets, urinals, and sinks should be mopped with a disinfectant. Shower walls should be scrubbed with a long handle sponge. Removal of hair from drains on a daily basis will help prevent clogging.

Carpeting used in playing areas should be vacuumed daily. In areas such as gymnasiums, large industrial type vacuums must be used in order to speed the cleaning process. Corners and carpet edges should be cleaned with a hand vacuum once a week. Inspection and treatment of stains should be done during daily vacuuming. Simple stain removal can be accomplished by applying warm soapy water with a sponge, working from the edges of the stain to the center. A mixture of vinegar, liquid detergent and water will dissolve common stains such as blood, vomitus and urine. Tougher stains may require a stronger solution such as cleaning fluid. If cleaning fluids are used they should be followed by an application of detergent and water. Long term maintenance of carpeting requires the use of a steam cleaner. This procedure should occur once a year.

Carpeting used in other areas such as offices and hallways should be maintained in much the same way. Frequency of cleaning depends on usage.

Walls

Melamine panels used in the construction of racquetball courts are highly resistant to dirt and are easily maintained. Frequency of use will determine how often they should be cleaned. A spray-on detergent applied with a sponge will remove most stains. Abrasive cleaners should never be used. Tougher stains may require using solvents. When these products are used, doors to courts should be left open for ventilation. After solvents are used, walls should be washed with soap and water. A battery-operated powered lift will facilitate upper walls and ceilings.

Racquetballs court walls constructed of fiberglass reinforced resin are cleaned in the same manner as melamine panels.

Saunas

Saunas, like locker rooms and public toilets, should be kept clean and odor-free at all times. Towels or mats should be used by participants at all times to prevent perspiration stains. Soft wood is used in the construction of saunas and is easily penetrated by perspiration. Stains caused by perspiration can be removed with a solution of warm soapy water and ammonia. If surfaces are badly stained, they may require sanding with a fine grain sand paper. Floors and walls of the sauna should be mopped with the same detergent used for cleaning the benches. The heater should be

wiped down with a damp rag once a week or as needed to remove dust. Saunas used daily should be cleaned at least once a week and should only be cleaned when not in use.

Swimming pools

Maintenance of swimming pools is more complicated and involved than maintenance of special surfaces and therefore should never be attempted without the services of an expert. Maintenance involves adhering to local and state ordinances as well as basic principles of pool chemistry and daily care. For information pertaining to maintenance of swimming pools seek advice from manufacturers, pool service companies as well as Certified Pool Operators.

Effective maintenance will extend the life of the facility and improve the morale of the user. Clean facilities encourage neatness, respect for property and make a strong and positive contribution to the wellness concept.

Selected Bibliography

Cut costs and win friends by planning or remodeling schools for easy maintenance. (1973, July). *Nations Schools, 92,* 36.

Floor Care from A to Z. (1986, October) *American school and university. 59,* 28-32.

Montgomery,B. (1985) Preparation of video tapes for use in orientation of custodial staff in recreation facilities. In Bailey,D., Greaves, E., Holsberry,W., & Reznik, J. (Eds.) *Management and rec sports.* Corvallis: NIRSA.

Nogradi, G. (1987, March). A systematic approach to facility maintenance. *Athletic Business*, pp.48-52.

Manufacturers and Distributors

Form Products
(Torpedo Cans)
P.O. Box 1520
Wausau, WI 54402

Genie Industries
Lifts
P.O. Box 69
Redmond,WA 98073-0069

Tennant Company
Power Sweepers
701 N. Lilac Dr.
minneapolis, MN 55440

Up-Right, Inc.
Lifts
1431 Industrial Dr.
Itasca, IL 60143

Bolotin
440 N. Mannheim Road
Hollside, IL 60162

Beginning
Operations

Developing Policies and Procedures

In developing policies and procedures a clear understanding of the purpose of each should be determined. Procedures are the actions needed to enforce the policies. Therefore, in terms of beginning operations for a recreation or fitness/wellness facility, policies must be developed prior to establishing procedures.

Policies are guidelines. They direct the organization's provision of services to clientele. Before establishing policies for a recreation or fitness/wellness facility, copies of policies from similar agencies or operations should be secured. These, along with input from persons who will be responsible for managing the facility, and from potential users will help in the development of these guidelines.

Whereas policies are developed primarily for the user, procedures are developed for those responsible for operation of the facility. For example a policy may read, "No turf shoes may be worn inside the facility." The corresponding procedure would read "Supervisors in charge of the facility will make rounds every hour checking for participants wearing turf shoes.

Any person wearing turf shoes will be asked to leave the building or change shoes."

After policies and procedures are established, they should be printed, bound in an attractive cover and made available to potential clientele prior to the opening of the new facility. They are crucial to the operations of the facility.

An outline to assist in developing a policies and procedures manual is presented in Appendix E.

Marketing

Marketing recreation and fitness/wellness programs involves identifying the consumer's needs and then delivering services to satisfy these needs. Marketing is a very strategic process. Strategies must be determined by available resources and with the realization that consumers' needs change. Those who provide leisure and fitness/wellness programs must be good listeners so they are aware when these needs change.

In defining the market in the "recreation and fitness/wellness business," we should consider all the members of the community who are potential users. In this particular case, nearly everyone comprises the potential market. Therefore, in developing strategies, everyone must be considered.

When considering a marketing strategy, two very important questions should be asked: What motivates people to participate in recreation and fitness/wellness programs, and what demotivates them?

Motivations to participate

•**Good impressions**. A competent staff and a well maintained, serviceable facility create a good impression.

•**Slogans**. Slogans or identifiable logos create awareness and consumers remember and associate programs with them. Tangible items, like t-shirts, mugs, key rings, etc. Bearing this slogan or logo further the awareness.

•**Convenience**. Services should be accessible as well as acceptable. Nearby parking and available locker facilities are examples of conveniences.

•**Promises**. Awards and recognition for participating or winning are extrinsic motivators that initiate a response in the participant.

De-motivations to participate

•**Poor handling** of the public and rudeness will create ill will with the participant.

•**Take-it-or-leave-it attitudes** will quickly be realized by the participant. Good marketing practices entail listening to the consumer's requests and striving to accommodate these wishes.

•**Unannounced closings and cancellations** rank high among demotivators. Closings and cancellations should be announced or posted well in advance.

•**Unkept, poorly maintained facilities** will discourage participation and likewise create an attitude of not caring among users. Users have a tendency to take better care of facilities that are well maintained.

These factors have a profound influence on the potential user. The mere fact that new facilities are built or old ones are renovated does not guarantee an overwhelming interest in their use. Those responsible for marketing must exert energy and spend time in applying basic marketing strategies.

Recreation and fitness/wellness services are marketed largely through people, however advertising is the means by which the consumer's interest is advanced. The first consideration in advertising is to catch the eye of the consumer. An excellent way to do this is to develop a logo that will be repeated time and again on all advertisements. This establishes a link with the audience and creates a professional image as well.

Next, a decision must be made regarding type of media used to reach the potential clientele. Printed materials, especially newspapers and magazines, are perhaps the most effective means of advertising. This approach is economical and reaches large numbers of local consumers. It is a relatively simple means of getting the word to the masses.

Broadcasting either on radio or television likewise reaches a large number of people but is much more expensive than using printed materials. Due to the high cost of air time, a limited amount of information can be disseminated.

Direct advertising through mailings, posted announcements, signs or billboards is effective but time consuming and expensive. Production time and costs may be limiting factors.

In advertising circles today, the argument is whether creativity or positioning is the most effective means of advancing the consumer's interest. The following is an example of creativity:

> *Creative Idea:* **A twenty-four hour telephone service for information regarding programs.**
> *Creative Results:*   REC CHECK: 555-1234.

Positioning, on the other hand, identifies the agency or organization with competitors or with other similar groups. For instance, "top rated fitness/wellness facilities," "the only facility in town with a separate free weight room," "the largest university sponsored race in the country" are all positioning phrases. Both creativity and positioning can contribute to the advertising efforts of the programmer.

Regardless of the choice, consideration should be given to cost and the number of consumers reached. Advertising requires money and should be a priority budget item.

The following suggestions will assist in developing effective marketing strategies:

• **Determine the objectives of the organization or agency.** Whether the primary objective of the organization programming within the facility is fitness, recreation for the aging, campus recreation, or community recreation, it should be clearly identified before marketing strategies begin.

• **Know the consumer.** In some cases the consumer will be many types of individuals ranging from infants to older adults whereas in other cases the majority of individuals will be of the same age, such as university students. The economic status of the consumer should also be considered.

• **Know the competition.** The competition may be the local YMCA, the local university, local health clubs, or the community recreation program. Regardless, before marketing plans are developed the completion should be analyzed.

• **Establish a network among professionals in the field.** Networking not only contributes to one's professional growth, it also is essential in marketing. Other professionals contribute new ideas and provide suggestions for success that can not be obtained from any other source.

• **Construct a good marketing plan.** Involve recreation program specialists, participants and other individuals that might contribute to the plan.

• **Be innovative; be original.** New and original ideas are always refreshing.

• **Give something away free**. The word "free" attracts a lot of attention, whether displayed in a store window, on a billboard or in a recreation facility. We all like to think we can get something free. "Freebies" can range from free membership to t-shirts. Regardless, they are a wonderful means of attracting attention.

• **Make the facility as attractive and convenient as possible.** Daily maintenance and upkeep will help to keep facilities attractive. Conveniences include attractive locker room facilities and accessible parking for clientele.

•**Reach as many people as possible through advertising**. As previously mentioned, effective advertising is a primary means of marketing a facility.

•**Train staff, especially in handling people.** Training is covered in another section of this chapter.

•**Never be satisfied or complacent.** Management that becomes satisfied or complacent will soon find themselves with a stagnant program and an outdated facility.

•**Capitalize on the benefits services will provide.** In the long run, consumers are actually buying the benefits and not the services. Answer the question, "What can utilizing your facility do for me?"

Selling the benefits of leisure an fitness/wellness programs is the key to success. The result is often in direct proportion to the effectiveness of the marketing strategies used.

Public Relations

Good public relations begin by caring for oneself, caring for others and caring about the facility and program where you work. Building personnel give the impression of caring for themselves when they dress neatly and appropriately for the type of work they do. They give the impression that they enjoy their work when they meet patrons with a smile and a friendly greeting.

A friendly greeting also lets patrons know that you care about them. Initiating a conversation or simply being a good listener

may determine whether or not someone returns to the facility. Patrons usually like to talk about their reason for being there and are actually seeking encouragement to return.

Individuals working in a recreation or fitness/wellness facility should be well informed about the facility and the programs housed within. Willingness to give patrons a tour will often encourage membership and participation.

Persons working in recreation and fitness/wellness facilities have a public relations job. In the course of a day many different types of individuals will enter. Each should be treated as special. The success of the programs housed within depends greatly on human relations skills These skills should become part of training for staff.

Training staff

Who should be trained? All employees responsible for supervision and/or maintenance of facility.

Inservice training

Hands on experience in proper use and apparatus is by far more effective than demonstrations alone. All employees responsible for setting up courts (tennis nets, badminton nets, etc.) should have an opportunity to carry through the operations from start to completion.

Training in administering cardio-pulmonary resuscitation (CPR) should be required of all persons working in recreation and fitness/wellness facilities. Numerous courses are taught in communities and schools on a regular basis. Ideally a member of the recreation or fitness/wellness staff will be certified to teach classes. CPR can be included as a program as well as a part of staff training.

Although all pool personnel must be certified by the American Red Cross in order to supervise water activities, they should also review policies and procedures for the facility where they will be supervising. "Hands on" orientation programs regarding location of life saving equipment, telephones and emergency exits are essential for training staff in the proper supervision of swimming pools.

As previously mentioned, learning to work with people is an essential skill of those responsible for supervising facilities. Proper greetings and the best intentions don't always ensure a happy patron, therefore working with people sometimes means working with angry people. They may be dissatisfied with the facility or the program or they may be upset with another patron. In either case, what they want is help. They want the person responsible to "fix it." Supervisory staff should be well trained in conflict resolution. This may require having an expert involved in the training process. It is well worth the investment to have staff properly trained in this area.

Maintenance staff should also receive special training in caring for any new surfaces that they may not be familiar with.

Employee handbook

An employee handbook should be available to all staff and should be available prior to inservice training programs. A sample

outline which may be used in developing guidelines is included in Appendix F.

Suggested Bibliography

Christopher, M. (1980) *Effective Marketing management*. Hants-England: Grover Publishing Co. Limited.

Cravens, D. (1982) *Strategic marketing*. Homewood, Il: Richard D. Irwin, Inc.

Appendix A

Sample Request for Statement of Interest and Qualifications

Memorandum to: Architects

Springfield Community College is studying the feasibility of constructing a recreation facility and is soliciting statements of interest and qualifications from a member of architectural firms. The architectural planning team will be used to assist with the following:

- Site selection and needs
- Determining financial needs
- Developing a financial program
- Securing constituency support
- Designing the facility
- Preparing plans and specifications
- Contract documents
- Supervising construction

Statements of interest and qualifications should be submitted to Director of Campus Recreation, Springfield Community College, U.S.A. not later than September 1, 1988. Proposals should include the following:

- Why your firm is interested
- Your firms experience with similar projects
- The qualifications of individuals working on the project
- References

All proposals will be reviewed and a short list will be developed by September 30, 1988. At least four firms will be invited to campus for an interview.

Appendix B

Sample
Request for Proposal
for the
Recreation Facility

by

SPRINGFIELD COMMUNITY COLLEGE

September, 1988

Introduction

Springfield Community College (SCC) has selected a committee to do a study to determine the feasibility of constructing a recreation facility to be located on the SCC campus.

General Information

Questions should be directed to:

Director of Campus Recreation
Springfield Community College
U.S.A.
(100) 555-0000

Deadline for Proposals

Six copies must be received no later than September 1, 1988.

Limitations of Liability

Springfield Community College assumes no responsibility or liabilty for costs incurred by proposers responding to this RFP or in responding to any further request for interviews, additional data, etc. prior to the issuance of a contract.

Rejection of Proposals

Springfield Community College reserves the right to reject any and all proposals if this is held to be in their best interest.

Proposal Evaluation

Each proposal will be reviewed by a committee based on the following criteria:

1. Firm's reputation and qualifications
2. Experience with similar projects
3. Ability of firm to meet project deadlines
4. Willingness to assume responsibility for this project
5. Estimated costs for each phase
6. Availability to begin

After all proposals have been received and evaluated several firms will be invited to the SCC campus for interviews. A combination of the evaluation of this document and the interview will be considered by the planning committee.

Format of Proposal

Submit six copies using the following format:
Resume of firm
Resume of persons who would be assigned to project
Work history of similar projects
Name, addresses and telephone number of clients
Summary of project
Start and completion date of work
Budget
Cost of preliminary work
Location of office where work will be performed
Conceptual design
Estimated cost of design
Other data that would be of value to the committee

Appendix C

Architect Evaluation

Preliminary Design and Budget

Name of Firm: _____

Rating 1-5 (1 being the lowest)

1. How long has the firm been under the present principals?
2. What experience has the firm had in the design of recreational facilities?
3. What experience has the firm had in the design of facilities for colleges and universities?
4. Is your firm involved in any litigation of any sort on any present or past projects as a result of design or construction problems?
5. Describe your in-house A/E staff; i.e. how many registered architects.?
6. Do you have in-house mechanical and electrical engineering staffs? Do you have in-house interior design staff?
7. Describe your staff and methods of preparing project estimates and/or budgets.
8. Describe your cost control procedure in order to work within fixed budget parameters. What is your track record for meeting budgets and time schedules over the past two years?
9. Describe your procedure to make preliminary design and realistic budgets for a project of this nature.
10. Describe your procedure to evaluate a program statement and to work within the framework of a program submitted by the user.
11. Is your present workload such that your firm could give this project top priority? Can we expect to get a "first team" approach as compared to lower echelon attention?
12. Describe a typical team to develop the preliminary design and budget for this project.
13. Describe your format for presentation of the required documentation for the project.

Appendix D

Evaluation Criteria

Name of Firm: _____

Rating 1-5, (1 being the lowest)   Comments

1. *Experience*
    a.   Athletic Facilities
    b.   Similar scope projects
    c.   Team participants

2. *Firm Capability*
    a.   Breadth of skills
    b.   Size/workload
    c.   Associates
    d.   Stability

3. *Organization*
    a.   Project team
    b.   Engineers
    c.   Consultants
    d.   Joint venture/affiliation

4. *Consistency*
    a.   Athletic facilities record
    b.   Quality control
    c.   Follow through

5. *Design*
    a.   Innovation
    b.   Aesthetics
    c.   Architectural and interior design
         engineering balance

6. *Program*
    a.   Function
    b.   Environment
    c.   Program
    d.   Budget

7.   *Engineering response*
   a.   Mechanical
   b.   Electrical
   c.   Structural

8.   *Budget*
   a.   Design to budget
   b.   Change orders
   c.   Attitudes
   d.   Schedule record

9.   *Balance*
   a.   Design
   b.   Engineering
   c.   Program
   d.   Budget

10.   *Design Philosophy*
   a.   Preparation
   b.   Balance

Suggested Outline for Developing a Policies Manual

I. Introduction
- A statement regarding functions of organzation, e.g. provide programming for certain populations, scheduling events in the facility, etc.

II. Facility Description
- A description of each area, e.g. weight/exercise room, racquetball courts, etc.

III. Building Access
- An explanation of control access if such applies.
- An explanation of penalty for violation of entry policy.
- An explanation of entry, exit and re-entry policies for joggers and users of outdoor facilities.

IV. General Facility Conduct
- A statement regarding use of tobacco, eating and drinking, gum chewing and consumption of alcoholic beverages.
- A statement regarding expectorating inside the facility.
- A statement concerning types of shoes permitted in facility.
- A statement concerning proper place and storage of bicycles.
- A statement pertaining to use of personal radios.
- The "lost and found" procedure.
- A statement regarding use of areas for designated purpose only, e.g. no soccer balls in racquetball courts.
- A priority use statement, e.g. scheduled tournaments have priority use of basketball courts, etc.
- A statement concerning courtesy, and safe use of the facility.
- A statement regarding accidents, the participants' resonsibility for reporting them, and the procedure for reporting them.

V. Authorized Use of Facility
- A description of each type of user and procedure for gaining entry to the facility, e.g. students must present a valid ID in order to gain admittance.

VI. User Fee Table

VII. Locker/Towel Rental Service
- A statement regarding procedure for short term and long term usage, including fees.
- A statement regarding repossession of locker space at end of term including penalty fee for not following procedure.

VIII.   Area Use
    • The rules of conduct for each area.
    • The reservation procedures for each area.

IX.   Rental Policies
    • The procedure for renting all or any part of facility.
    • The cost for renting all or any part of facility.
    • A suggested formula follows for determining rental costs.

rate x hours x volume = _____ + _____ (personnel costs) = TOTAL COST

How to determine volume:
    1-50 persons = 1
    51-100 persons = 1.25
    101-200 persons = 1.50
    201+   persons = 1.75

X.   Equipment Check Out
    • The procedure for borrowing equipment.

(Suggested outline for use in developing policies manual, courtesy of Northern Illinois University.)

Appendix F

Outline for Employee Handbook

I. *General Information*

    A.   Tax information
    B.   Pay checks
    C.   Inservice training requirements
    D.   Employees ID Cards
    E.   Appropriate attire
    F.   Sign-in procedure
    G.   Break procedure
    H.   Sick and substitution procedure
    I.   Suspension policy and procedure
    J.   Evaluation procedure

II. *Emergency care procedure*

III. *Job responsibilities*

- Description of each position - responsibilities prior to opening facility; work procedure and closing procedure.

IV. *Appendix*

- Samples of all forms used, e.g. accident forms, space requisition forms, daily requirements.
- Emergency procedures for fire, tornadoes, etc.

(Used at Northern Illinois University, Office of Campus Recreation, DeKalb, IL)

Glossary

Anchored channel: Type of floor installation in which hardwood is held together with steel clips and mounted in channel tracks.

Anchored sleeper: Type of floor installation in which hardwood is nailed to a sleeper which is placed over a concrete base.

Ceiling membrane: A surface which defines the upper boundaries of an enclosed space.

Ceramic tile: Brittle tile, made of clay fired in a high temperature kiln.

Circuit training: A type of exercise course utilizing weight machines and other equipment or apparatus interspersed with equipment and apparatus used for aerobic benefit.

CMU: Concrete masonry unit; concrete blocks.

Cuspidor: Receptacle located adjacent to a water fountain; used for expectorating.

Direct lighting: Presentation of light in which beam shines directly on an object.

Double glazing: Two window panes with air space between them; space in between helps insulate.

Drywall: Gypsum boards; sheet of plaster faced on both sides with paper; common household wall.

Eye wash: Eye solution kept in areas where strong chemicals are used.

Fitness/wellness facility: A facility which promotes activities which contribute to total well-being of the individual.

Floating sleeper: Type of floor installation where a softwood subfloor is placed between the sleeper and the hardwood.

Fluorescent lighting: Light source created by ionization which produces ultraviolet rays causing them to strike a phosphorous tube.

Footcandle: A unit of illuminance in an area one foot from a uniform source of light from one candle.

Melamine laminated panel:	Molded panels made of plastic type material used in wall construction, eg. racquetball courts.
Mercury vapor lighting:	Type of high intensity discharge lighting in which the charge takes place through mercury vapor.
Metal halide lighting:	Type of high intensity discharge lighting, similar to mercury vapor except that the metal halide contains some metallic additives. The arc tube is also smaller than those in mercury lamps.
Plenum space:	Area between the underside of the floor/roof construction and the ceiling membrane.
Pneumatic resistance weight machine:	Apparatus equipped with hydraulic canister which determines resistance.
Poured in place flooring:	Liquid urethane surface poured over a concrete base.
Pre cast concrete:	Concrete cast in a mold to determine a specific shape before being placed in its final position.
PVC:	Polyvinylchloride; prefabricated vinyl flooring.
Quarry tile:	Tile made of stone.
Recreation facility:	A facility which provides opportunity for participating in leisure time pursuits.
Rolled surface:	Synthetic flooring manufactured in sheets and shipped in rolls; pre-fabricated.
Set up area:	Area adjacent to outdoor equipment centre. Used for setting up tents and checking other equipment such as sleeping bags, stoves, etc.
Sleeper:	Cushiony material used in installation of hardwood floors to provide a shock absorbing surface.
Sodium vapor lighting:	High intensity discharge lighting similar to metal halide and sodium vapor in which the arc tube is smaller and which contains no starting electrode inside.
Terrazzo tile:	Flooring made from marble or granite set in mortar and polished.